This New Man A Discourse in Portraits

Portrait of Benjamin Rush painted by Thomas Sully in 1812. Lent by Mr. and Mrs. Benjamin Rush.

Edited by J. BENJAMIN TOWNSEND

and introduced by CHARLES NAGEL

With an essay by OSCAR HANDLIN

This New Man

A Discourse in Portraits

Published for the National Portrait Gallery by the Smithsonian Institution Press
City of Washington 1968

Smithsonian Publication 4752

Distributed by Random House, Inc.,
in the United States and Canada

Library of Congress Catalog 68-8535

Designed by Stephen Kraft
Printed by Vinmar Lithographing Company

A Different National Portrait Gallery

At first glance, the courage of the Board of Regents of the Smithsonian Institution in accepting the task of setting up a National Portrait Gallery can be measured only by mega-scale — *mega*-watts, *mega*-meters, or *mega*-tons. To found a portrait gallery in the 1960s — when American portraiture has already reached the zenith in price and the nadir in supply, when the museums and halls of legislature of this country already possess most of the available portraits and sculpture of famous personages and are little likely to release them to a johnny-come-lately — seems an act of bravery indeed.

The positive nature of the act of the Regents is further evoked by the composition of the National Portrait Gallery Commission. Scholars are preponderant on that Commission, and it is therefore an earnest of policy and plans to come. It is quite obvious that this National Portrait Gallery, in the very act of being created when it was, has already set its sights on being a *different* National Portrait Gallery. Scholarly it must be, concentrating on a dimension in historical biography and iconography largely left uncharted by the great historical and biographical source books of this nation. The opportunity is here, if it can be correctly measured, for setting forth on a series of profound and seminal catalogues and historical studies in the field of likenesses of American personages, never before marshalled or planned as a whole. Few tasks in American historical scholarship could be more challenging. The Gallery should be a center, as well, for original biographical studies by those historians, who just might happen to be interested in human beings rather than social institutions.

The second great purpose of this Gallery created in the 1960s is to explore all possible means of educating the visiting public in experiencing the personages that are to be portrayed. The small permanent collections of formal portraits and sculptures can be buttressed with carefully chosen changing exhibits along thematic lines and surrounded further with a total environment of accessories of every sort, including films, filmstrips, tapes, and objects designed to reproduce in kinetic fashion the lost atmosphere of the personality, to quicken the senses and thus to teach, objectively and without didacticism, some of the meaning of the times and of the world in which the personages lived.

If the National Portrait Gallery is to live up to its bold challenges, it must become one of the most exciting environments for scholars and the public alike in our Capital City.

S. DILLON RIPLEY
Secretary, Smithsonian Institution

Contents

1 **Introduction**

6 **"This Promiscuous Breed" —**
Sources of Diversity in the American Character
by Oscar Handlin

24 **The American Is Restless and Mobile**

Explorers
Nathaniel Bowditch, William Clark, Albert Einstein,
Robert Hutchins Goddard, Meriwether Lewis, Robert Millikan,
Charles Wilkes

Frontiersmen and Expansionists
Francis Asbury, Daniel Boone, John Charles Frémont,
Sam Houston, Matthew C. Perry, William H. Seward,
John A. Sutter, Brigham Young

Immigrants and Expatriates
Alexander Graham Bell, August Belmont, John Singleton Copley,
Albert Gallatin, Alexander Hamilton, Henry James, Richard Lee,
Joseph Priestley, Joseph Pulitzer, Augustus Saint-Gaudens,
Carl Schurz, Gertrude Stein, Theodore Thomas,
James Abbot McNeill Whistler

57 **The American Is a Citizen and Sovereign**

Lawmakers
Sir William Berkeley, Charles Calvert, John Hancock,
Charles Evans Hughes, James Kent, Henry Cabot Lodge,
John Marshall, Frederick Augustus Conrad Muhlenberg,
Roger Sherman, Charles Sumner, Daniel Webster

Liberators and Crusaders
Samuel Adams, Dorothea Lynde Dix, Frederick Douglass,
James Cardinal Gibbons, Horace Greeley, Harry L. Hopkins,
Tadeusz Andrzej Bonawentura Kościuszko, Marquis de Lafayette,
Lucretia Coffin Mott, Thomas Paine, John J. Pershing

Defenders and Peacemakers
Jeffery Amherst, John C. Calhoun, Henry Clay, Stephen Decatur,
Nathanael Greene, John Paul Jones, Robert E. Lee,
Oliver Hazard Perry, Elihu Root, Winfield Scott,
William Tecumseh Sherman, Sitting Bull

97   The American Is a Rebel and Nonconformist

Charles Brockden Brown, Aaron Burr, Cadwallader Colden,
Jefferson Davis, Eugene V. Debs, Ralph Waldo Emerson,
H. L. Mencken, Osceola, Albert Pinkham Ryder,
Henry David Thoreau

108   The American Is Practical

Amateurs and Versatilists
Willam Cullen Bryant, DeWitt Clinton, Benjamin Franklin,
Edward Hicks, Samuel F. B. Morse, Charles Willson Peale,
Paul Revere, Royall Tyler

Inventors and Innovators
Mathew B. Brady, John Dewey, Robert Fulton, Henry George,
William James, Adolf Meyer, Eugene O'Neill, Edgar Allan Poe,
Benjamin Rush, Benjamin Silliman, Louis H. Sullivan,
Eli Whitney

Inquirers
Louis Agassiz, John James Audubon, George Washington Carver,
Matthew Maury, Albert Michelson, David Rittenhouse

139   The American Is an Organizer

Rugged Individualists
John Jacob Astor, Andrew Carnegie, George Eastman,
Thomas A. Edison, Marshall Field, Henry Ford, Jay Gould,
Mark Hanna, William Randolph Hearst, James J. Hill,
Andrew Mellon, Mrs. Potter Palmer, Sir Walter Raleigh,
John D. Rockefeller, Cornelius Vanderbilt

Altruists
Jane Addams, Clara Barton, Joseph Brant,
Charles Richard Drew, Samuel Gompers,
The Mayo Brothers, William White

165   The American Finds God in Divers Ways

John Carroll, William Ellery Channing, Mary Baker Eddy,
Jonathan Edwards, Increase Mather, Dwight L. Moody,
Joseph Smith, Isaac Mayer Wise

174   The American Is Larger than Life

Phineas T. Barnum, William Jennings Bryan,
William Lloyd Garrison, Thomas Nast, Will Rogers,
Harriet Beecher Stowe, Mark Twain

183   The American Seeks an Identity

Interpreters and Imagemakers
David Belasco, George Bellows, Charles Bulfinch, George Catlin,
James Fenimore Cooper, Thomas Eakins, Stephen Collins Foster,
Nathaniel Hawthorne, Sinclair Lewis,
Henry Wadsworth Longfellow, Herman Melville,
John Philip Sousa, Walt Whitman, Florenz Ziegfeld

Idols
Buffalo Bill Cody, Charlotte Cushman, George Armstrong Custer,
Edwin Forrest, Jean Harlow, Fiorello La Guardia, Lillian Russell,
Babe Ruth, John L. Sullivan, Jim Thorpe, Rudolph Valentino

Introduction

On the occasion of our formal introduction to the public, after many years of planning, it seems wise to set down a few of the limitations within which the National Portrait Gallery will have to function in carrying out its mission as charged by the Congress.

First, ours must never be regarded as a gallery of art but rather as a history museum, one with a serious national purpose. Consequently, the sitter is always the most important element to be kept in mind, particularly when likenesses are being selected for the collections. Naturally, every effort will be made to secure as fine portraits aesthetically as are available, on the principle that generally an excellent portrait will also be an outstanding work of art. But a genuine likeness taken from life is the primary consideration. In rare cases, where the archetype simply is not to be had, a replica or a fine copy of an original life portrait will be deemed acceptable. The portrait of the late President John F. Kennedy in our collection is a case in point. Furthermore, no likeness save that of a President and his wife may be exhibited, except temporarily, until the sitter has been ten years deceased.

Next, it should be remembered with charity that, although the idea of such a gallery is as old as the Republic, the National Portrait Gallery is off to a late start. It follows that a great many portraits, particularly those of the Founding Fathers, have found their way to the walls of other institutions and are not available to us, save as temporary loans as in the present exhibition.

Finally, we are not yet an institution that has at its disposal large funds for purchase. This is a considerable handicap, since portraits of great interest, particularly of early figures related to American history, come on the market relatively seldom, usually at short notice, and often at prices that are beyond us. We hope, therefore, that gifts of money for acquisitions and of portraits in any medium will soon begin to appear — gifts that will enable us to carry out to the fullest extent our avowed purpose of exhibiting, free to the public, a collection of the likenesses of men and women in all walks of life who have contributed to the history and culture of the United States of America from the times of the earliest colonies to the present. Not every one appearing on our walls will be a hero. A fine likeness of Aaron Burr, for instance, would be as welcome as our bust of Alexander Hamilton; and one of John Wilkes Booth — not so important, perhaps, but just as interesting — might in its own way prove as desirable as our well-known portrait of Abraham Lincoln.

To the donors to the Gallery's collections, who have shown a really prophetic generosity, we are profoundly grateful. Outstanding among our early gifts are thirty-two likenesses which were assigned to us by the National Gallery of Art, including twenty-three that came to us through testamentary instruction of the late Andrew Mellon. The likeness of Pocahontas, an early seventeenth-century English portrait, is one of the great treasures of this group. Another welcome gift, with happy implications of sentiment, is the four satiric watercolor drawings of Americans presented to us by the Trustees of our distinguished prototype, the National Portrait Gallery of London. Meanwhile, our collections to date still number only a little better than 500 items. This gives an idea of what remains to be done in terms of acquisition. Many activities ancillary to the collection — such as a formal education program, the preparation of filmstrips, slides, and reproductions for the museum shop, the building up of our biographical and iconographical records, and, finally, a program of research and publication — will be undertaken as soon as funds permit.

So we begin our new life as a museum, within the large Smithsonian complex of such organizations, not aping any other institution but following modestly and optimistically in the great tradition of the portrait galleries of Dublin, Edinburgh, and London. At the same time, we regard our fundamental purpose as differing from European models just as the life and relatively brief history of our country differ from theirs. We are fortunate in occupying a portion of one of the most impressive and venerable structures in Washington, the Old Patent Office, a building begun in 1836; and we salute the many who had a part in its preservation and modernization. Our galleries here are up-to-date and well equipped. For this we are beholden to our architects and to the Congress, which assigned this building to the Smithsonian Institution for our use.

After a long, hazardous pilgrimage we have come finally to our premier exhibition, *This New Man: A Discourse in Portraits*. The title and central theme are taken from Michel-Guillaume Jean de Crèvecoeur (1735-1813): "What then is the American, this new man?" (*Letters from an American Farmer*, 1782). Crèvecoeur was a French emigrant of distinguished ancestry who, after serving under Montcalm in Canada, traveled widely in that country and in the American Colonies. In 1769 he settled on a farm in Orange County, New York, and during the next decade composed vivid essays on contemporary American frontier life, economic forces, and social conditions. As if to bear out his own observation that the American is a composite of many races and cultures, he signed these essays "J. Hector St. John." Crèvecoeur's question as to the identity of the American has been repeated often in the past by celebrated spokesmen — both American and foreign — but perhaps never more often than it is today.

The traditional mode for defining the American genius, of course, is as a study of opposites, with the Virgin and Dynamo of Henry Adams as its classic form. It soon became apparent to the organizers of *This New Man* that classifying American personalities according to dichotomies — pragmatists against idealists, expansionists against regionalists, individualists against conformists — would have reduced the American to botanic classification and answered a riddle with a mere paradox. A less sophisticated and arbitrary formula was sought.

To offer simpler answers and to avoid a merely chronological arrangement, our exhibition makes a number of statements about the American character — most of them obvious and unassailable enough; some, we trust, more provocative. Each of these statements is illustrated by a group or groups of portraits, for the most part arranged according to the sitter's primary interest or contribution. Each group of portraits, or in some instances each series of groups, seeks to answer the central question by presenting a single facet of the national character. For example, after the question "What is the American?" and the statement

"He is restless and mobile" come three categories of sitters to document that statement — explorer, frontiersman and expansionist, and immigrant and expatriate. By arranging the sitters according to type or predominant interest, a wide spectrum of American talent and energy is presented. And by answering the central question each time by a fresh statement, the visitor or reader is allowed to sample the exhibition or progress conscientiously as he chooses.

Several caveats are in order. The polarists have a point: In endeavoring to communicate clearly and directly to a general public our exhibition is not so simplistic as to ignore that for every statement one makes about the American, one can safely say the opposite. And by no means have we been able to examine all our national traits — positive or negative. Furthermore, it is clear that many sitters included to illustrate one trait could have been used with equal validity to illustrate one or more other traits. Benjamin Franklin, for instance, who appears as an "amateur and versatilist," could with the same propriety have appeared as a "defender and peacemaker," an "inventor and innovator" or "inquirer," an "organizer," an "individualist," or an "interpreter."

The Gallery's exhibition committee at the outset laid down certain ground rules which may explain the absence of some obvious exemplars and popular favorites. The committee decided that wherever possible only likenesses from life would be accepted and that no sitter who had not been deceased for ten years should be included. Portraits were selected primarily for the sitter's importance and relevance to the theme of the show. While we have been phenomenally successful on the whole in borrowing for this opening exhibition, it should be remembered that the definitively fine portrait was not always available. Finally, in organizing the exhibition the staff attempted to demonstrate not only the diversity of the American character but something of the variety of media — from oil painting and sculpture to watercolor, pastel, and charcoal drawing to graphic prints and posters to daguerreotype and photograph — in which American portraiture has appeared. But whether one considers the content of *This New Man* or its technical features, we hope that the viewer will bear in mind that it is subtitled *A Discourse in Portraits* — that at our own hazard we have invited the visitor himself to be a major participant and that the exhibition is quite intentionally open-ended and unfinished.

Our opening exhibition, running from 7 October through 31 December 1968, is largely the result of great generosity on the part of individuals and of sister institutions, both here and abroad. It represents a general willingness to share with us a wealth of collections that has come to them through many years. We hope that their good fortune will gradually come to be true of us as well, now that we have begun to function and at last become visible to the public.

This bow to the public could not have been achieved without the loyal and assiduous participation of the entire Gallery staff. The exhibition was conceived and organized by Virginia C. Purdy, Keeper of the Catalogue of American Portraits, and J. Benjamin Townsend, Assistant Director of the Gallery. The portraits were researched and assembled by the Curator's staff under the direction of the Curator, Robert G. Stewart. Daniel J. Reed, Historian, Mrs. Purdy, and their assistants, with the aid of other specialists in American history and culture, prepared the text. The specialists consulted were Professor Clarence C. Goen, Wesley Seminary, Washington, D. C.; Professors James E. O'Neill and James L. Penick, Jr., Loyola University, Chicago; and Professor Martin Pops, State University of New York at Buffalo. I am deeply grateful to the staff and to those outside it who have helped in realizing so signally our opening exhibition.

In the present exhibition the portraits within each group appear chronologically by subjects' birthdates; in the table of contents the names are in alphabetical order within each group. Dimensions are given in inches, height preceding width. All information on the portraits and designations of ownership have been supplied by the lenders. Where no date is available for a work the editor has supplied "not dated." Except where indicated otherwise, all photographs reproduced in this book are by the National Portrait Gallery or the lender of the portrait.

CHARLES NAGEL, Director
National Portrait Gallery

"This Promiscuous Breed"

Sources of Diversity in the American Character

On 4 July 1776, after the Declaration of Independence had been signed, the Continental Congress asked John Adams, Benjamin Franklin, and Thomas Jefferson to design a great seal for the United States. It was almost six years before the Congress made a final decision about this matter; and only one of the suggestions by the first distinguished committee survived — the motto. Jefferson, Adams, and Franklin had wished the national arms to be emblematic of the countries from which the new republic had been peopled and of the states of which it was composed. The motto was to describe the characteristic that had made the country what it was: *E Pluribus Unum* — out of many, one.

In choosing that phrase, the original committee expressed pride in a revolution which had not only cast off the restraints of empire but at the same time had forged a republic in which men were united, yet remained free. Thirteen separate colonies, not previously related except in their common subjection to Britain, had formed a single nation despite differences of climate, culture, and economy that continued to divide them. The great planters of South Carolina, the merchants of Philadelphia, and the farmers of Massachusetts were Congregationalists, Anglicans, Baptists, and Catholics, and were descended from Englishmen, Frenchmen, and Germans. They were fighting a bitter war to protect their liberty and to fashion a united government, yet without sacrificing their individuality.

In the almost two hundred years that have followed, the motto *E Pluribus Unum* has retained its meaning under circumstances that even Jefferson could not have anticipated. During this time the nation spread to its continental limits and beyond; it received millions of immigrants from every part of the world; its people left the farms for the cities as its economy shifted from an agricultural to an industrial base. Yet, except for one brief period, the United States retained its unity, while the new conditions did not extinguish the particular characteristics of its component parts. Its people remained many, but when it mattered the many could act as one.

That is why American society has always been difficult to understand and to describe. There is a national character and a national culture; Americans who meet each other in travel at home or abroad recognize their kinship whether they hail from Maine or Oregon. Yet the Georgian and the Rhode Islander do not speak alike; and the cut of a Texan's clothing is not that of a Bostonian's. A Baptist is not likely to be moved by the church in which a Catholic worships; nor do the Italian-American and the Negro respond to the same music. The Yankee lobsterman, the Polish auto worker, the reservation Navaho, and the Amish farmer are all Americans, yet they are strikingly different. Free institutions permit them to live side by side while remaining themselves and cooperating at points of mutual advantage.

St. John Crèvecoeur (1735-1813), French-born commentator on American frontier life and social forces, early perceived the effects of diversity when he asked the penetrating question, "What then is the American, this new man?" He gave his own answer, "*He* is an American, who, leaving behind him all his ancient prejudices and manners, receives new ones from the new mode of life he has embraced. . . . Here individuals of all nations are melted into a new race of men, whose labors and posterity will one day cause great changes in the world."

Since Crèvecoeur's day, observers speculating about the American character have generally agreed that a new type of man emerged in the New World. They have pointed to the restless and nomadic quality of American life, to its competitiveness and acquisitiveness, and to the paradox of rebellious individualism among people who pride themselves upon their citizenship; and they have often sought an explanation of those traits in the diversity of society in the United States. Undoubtedly there is some connection between the historic experiences of this heterogeneous nation and the personality of its people. To understand that connection it is necessary first to examine the sources of diversity, then to assess the effects of this diversity upon American social and cultural institutions, and finally to suggest the consequences for national character.

The diversity of Americans derived from two of the basic conditions of historic development in the United States. The country was so large and the environment so varied that regional differences exerted a powerful influence upon the organization of life and the patterns of behavior. Futhermore, the population, drawn from many parts of the earth, long retained the imprint of its heterogeneous heritage. As a result, regional and ethnic distinctions both played a continuing role in social and cultural development.

The American region was not one with precise boundaries that could be neatly drawn on a map and the fate of which nature had determined once and for all. Some observers might plausibly suppose that New England's rocky hills forced it to turn to manufacturing, or that Alabama's climate thrust it into the plantation system — plausibly but inaccurately. That mechanical view of the influence of geography on human character does not fully take into account the changes that man and his institutions effected. To the Indian the falls of the Merrimack River were an obstacle; to the Yankee planning a textile mill they were an opportunity. The black soil of Alabama revealed its value only after the Lancashire factories created a demand for cotton.

The region, therefore, was a complex entity. Its boundaries were set by all the elements that created a distinctive context for the life of the people who inhabited it. Its characteristics emanated from the interplay of land, people, and the circumstances of settlement — each working upon the other in the course of history.

The land occupied by the American people displayed the most diverse physical features. Its climate ranged from the near tropical in Hawaii and along the coast of the Gulf of Mexico to the near arctic in the northern Great Plains and Alaska. The geographers' designation "temperate" for the zone in which the nation lay meant not that temperatures were moderate but rather that they were subject to sharp seasonal variations. Uneven also was the quality of the soil, ranging from the rocky hills of New England and the bleak deserts of Nevada to the fertile plains of Minnesota and the rich alluvial deposits of the Mississippi Delta. Rainfall in the coastal areas was generally adequate; and much of the country east of the Mississippi could count on an average annual precipitation of more than twenty-five inches a year. But residents of the West for the most part had to accommodate themselves to conditions of semi-aridity. So long as agriculture was central to the life of the nation, these factors were critical.

The physiographic configuration of the country also affected the flow of population, the course of trade, and the situation of industry. The extensive systems of rivers and lakes long provided the most important means of moving goods and people. For more than a century the Mississippi and its links to the Great Lakes nurtured in the French hope for an empire that would stretch from Quebec to New Orleans. The same trade route in the nineteenth century sustained the prosperity of Chicago and St. Louis, just as the Hudson River sustained that of New York and as the Ohio did for Pittsburgh and Cincinnati. The natural inland waterways also influenced the lines of the canals and of the railroads, which at first supplemented the canals and then supplanted them. The location of water-power, forests, and deposits of iron ore, coal, and oil also helped men select the sites on which factories were to appear.

The land and its resources, however, were not static; they responded to the pressures of the economy and the effects of human occupation. The careless farmer as well as the axeman who leveled the forests could create deserts; and through irrigation, reforestation, and scientific methods of agriculture man could restore the soil. The Great Plains were considered unsuitable for farming until the invention of the steel plow enabled men to break the hard surface and until the reaper and the harvester helped them gather up the abundant yields of grain. Generally, the falls that marked the points at which rivers ceased to be navigable were attractive locations for cities, but improvements in the river channels and the building of canals and railroads altered the initial routes of transportation. Louisville, on the falls of the Ohio, could not depend on nature alone in order to compete with Cincinnati and Pittsburgh. On the Pacific coast, the increase in population created man-made problems of water scarcity and smog. The land's untouched wealth was hidden, and the realization of its potential was to depend on the wisdom or stupidity, the avarice or prudence, of the men who settled on it.

In 1600 the vast, empty land of America offered an exciting invitation to newcomers, and in the three centuries that followed the American population grew much more through immigration than through the increase of the original settlers. Multitudes came from Europe, where they had been uprooted by political, economic, and social changes. The first shocks were felt in the seventeenth century; the cumulative reverberations did not cease until well into the twentieth. A modernized agriculture in the Old World helped sustain the factory system, leaving both peasant and artisan without a livelihood. People fled from their villages and farms to the cities or overseas, hastened on their way by recurrent famines. Transformations in politics and culture accelerated the movement. The appearance of large centralized national states weakened the force of local particularism; and new ways of thought sapped the strength of custom and tradition so that men grew willing to try the unknown and to risk dangerous new undertakings.

The effects were felt first in England, the country from which the great majority of American colonists had been drawn. The flow from England continued through the nineteenth century, but meanwhile other elements were participating in the movement to America. The effects of change in England rippled through its borderlands, and the number of Welsh, Scots, and Irish immigrating to the United States increased after 1800.

On the continent of Europe, Germany was the first country in which the shock of modernization set large numbers of peasants in motion. The advance parties who had arrived before the Revolution were joined after 1830 by a steadily growing army of compatriots. In the decades that followed, the Scandinavian nations also lost part of their populations to America.

In the last quarter of the nineteenth century the countries of eastern and southern Europe added to the influx of American immigrants. Millions of peasants left the villages of the Austrian, Russian, and German empires and of Greece and Italy. They came to America along with numerous Jews, Armenians, and other peoples who had lived in the same societies. By then, too, smaller contingents from China and Japan had joined the migration.

Similar forces of modernization operated in all the places from which immigrants came. Yet each area had a culture uniquely its own. The villagers of Ireland and the Ukraine, of Sweden and Sicily, spoke different languages, worshiped according to different rituals, followed different routines of farming, and were bound by different habits of dress and diet. The ways of life they brought with them would yield gradually to the effects of the American environment; but these ways would subtly influence the American character.

The transfer of population from Africa to the New World followed a distinctive course. This was an involuntary migration, the result of the trade in men from the sub-Saharan regions that began before the end of the seventeenth century. The Africans brought to America occupied a status radically different from that occupied by the Europeans; and the institution of slavery was to shape for many generations the adjustment of Negroes to the world about them. Nevertheless, the cultural heritage of the Africans was also to have an enduring effect upon life in the United States.

Following a hiatus caused by the Revolution and the Napoleonic wars, immigration resumed after 1815 and reached a peak of 400,000 in 1854. This wave, which ended at the Civil War, brought some 7½ million persons to the United States. A second wave, between 1860 and 1890, brought about 8 million more. The crest came between 1890 and 1924 when more than 20 million newcomers swelled the population of the United States. Thereafter immigration subsided under the pressures of restrictive legislation, depression, and war.

The impact of the movement from overseas was always most intense in the eastern part of the country. The effects, however, spread throughout the continent, as the American population was continually redistributing itself. The results are seen in the nation's diversified culture and the restlessness of Americans.

Internal migration was characteristic of American life from the very start. Even in the seventeenth century, when the newly formed settlements were still fragile and when the leaders looked with disfavor on any shifts in the population, the adventurous and discontented emerged from the security of the stockades to try their own luck in the West. Later, as the danger from the Indians and from the hostile French and Spaniards abated, the pace westward accelerated. Determined families left the coasts and the river valleys to plunge into the interior. The Revolution threw open the region north of the Ohio River, an area that had long been the subject of conflict between France and Great Britain. Now American, this land received a steady flow of newcomers, particularly after the War of 1812, which had ended the danger of attack from Canada.

Internal migration developed specialists in movement. Fur traders, miners, and woodsmen were the first to penetrate beyond the line of settlement. Following them were pioneer farmers, intrepid and eager to take the chance of a lucky strike. These people were the cutting edge of the westward movement. Behind them advanced an army of more permanent residents. Families who had become impatient with the limited opportunities of the East settled on the partially cleared land. Then came the builders, merchants, speculators, lawyers, doctors, and ministers who created societies behind the frontier.

Between 1820 and 1860 the line of settlement shifted from the Alleghenies to across the Mississippi, and an outpost appeared on the Pacific coast. Three distinct elements were involved in this migration. Yankees moved through New York State across northern Ohio, Indiana, and Illinois to Iowa and Wisconsin. Southerners passed by way of Kentucky through the lower counties of the Northwest Territory into Missouri or through Tennessee to Alabama, Louisiana, and Texas. Immigrants from Europe, who generally remained for a time in the eastern cities, followed westward the earlier Americans who were more adept at living in the wilderness. Meanwhile, the discovery of gold in 1848 touched off the settlement of California.

Between the Civil War and World War I the westward flow of people mounted in volume as a network of railways helped spread the settlers across the continent. Alaska and Hawaii, having become American, also received newcomers, and all the while there was a steady movement to the cities from the farms and rural communities.

The forms of migration changed after World War I. The flow from the Old World slackened. Refugees who came in the 1930s and 1940s supplied the only significant number of newcomers from Europe. Now the migration had become almost entirely internal, but it was not of the frontier type, as earlier. Rather, the movement came in response to new opportunities arising from a mature economy. From the 1920s on, many Southerners — both blacks and whites — and others who no longer could "make a go of it," or who were tired of the effort to do so, moved northward and westward to the burgeoning metropolitan centers.

Although the constant reshuffling of population kept the country united, it also kept it from becoming homogeneous. No area or group was so detached that it could preserve its character through inertia; yet, the mobility encouraged the development of regional and ethnic cultures and associations to meet the needs of the members. Regions and ethnic groupings were not simply the static products of geography; they were defined by their histories. Fluid yet distinctive regional and ethnic interests and attitudes influenced the nation's political, cultural, and social institutions and the character of its people.

The way in which two regions were developed will serve to illustrate the pattern. New England was the first area to acquire an identity of its own. Its topography discouraged large-scale agriculture; its long coastline offered attractive bases for overseas trade; and its swift streams provided a foothold for manufacturing. Puritanism, the dominant cultural force during New England's first two centuries, played an equally important part in the development of the regional character. The community church, organized in autonomous congregations by many small farmers and a few great merchants, was a powerful instrument of social discipline, welding its members to a tight code of behavior and to an awareness of the obligations of conscience. Here, too, the town meeting laid a foundation for political democracy.

Finally, nineteenth-century New England was the setting for a literary renaissance. The generation of Emerson and Thoreau believed it could make man free and perfect through reform; and abolition, education, and temperance commanded its attention and support. Even then, however, industrialization and urbanization were altering the character of the region. By 1900 manufacturing had far outdistanced agriculture in importance, and a majority of the population, housed in cities, consisted of immigrants, many of them Catholics and Jews culturally distant from the old stock. The region had changed dramatically during the nineteenth century, yet it was visibly the product of its past.

History also shaped the character of the South, where the decisive element was not geography but the evolving relationship between white man and black man. Slavery had appeared in tidewater Virginia and Maryland before the opening of the eighteenth century; yet, neither there nor in North Carolina, Kentucky, and most of Tennessee — where settlement occurred later — were the physical features of the land propitious for large-scale agriculture. A substantial number of free white men, therefore, always cultivated their own farms. Theirs were the ideals that Jefferson expressed, and they were the pioneers who moved westward with the frontier, developing in the process the basic outlook of Jacksonian democracy. It was from this stock that Abraham Lincoln sprang.

The agricultural development of the Deep South began later and followed a different pattern. Settlement began in South Carolina toward the very end of the seventeenth century, and it did not begin in Georgia until after 1730, and in Alabama, Florida, and Mississippi until after 1820. It was in these states that the plantation system was most developed and the percentage of Negro slaves largest. Here even the poor whites of the hill country acquired a firm attachment to the values of the traditional cavalier South. Ironically, this society reached its peak in the decade just before the Civil War which was to destroy it. Its economy was then strong, vigorous, and expansive; and the dominant groups, determined to defend their way of life, welcomed secession and fought vigorously throughout the Civil War.

The sectional conflict, which led to secession, the war itself, and the aftermath of reconstruction, cemented regional ties through the force of a common experience. At first, the border states were torn by conflicting loyalties; they had to decide whether their future lay with freedom or slavery, with the yeoman or the planter. The decision was less difficult in the states of the lower South. The shocks of defeat and of the frustrated effort at reconstruction pulled the whole region together and preserved its unity into the twentieth century. For almost a hundred years, the South tried to preserve the spirit of slavery, even though the force of federal arms had destroyed its legal basis. The results were economic backwardness, a perversion of democratic processes, and a racial tension that ultimately was to affect the whole country. Yet the process established the South as a region — the "solid" South.

Other regions of the country also acquired particular characters through the interplay of land and people. The characteristics of the Middle West, the Great Plains, and the Pacific coast were the products of historic encounters of man and environment. Each of these regions achieved a distinctive identity, yet each was recognizable as part of the national whole.

Ethnic groupings were no more static than regional boundaries. The associations within which Americans organized their lives also took form through the play of historic influences that made people aware of differences of three distinct kinds: the move from the place of one's birth — or even the memory of an ancestral move — induced Kentuckians in Ohio, Yankees in California, Italians in New York to act together; the color of Negroes, Indians, Chinese separated these peoples from others; and distinctive creeds and practices kept Catholics, Baptists, Jews, and Mormons from worshiping together. Insofar as they separated people these differences sometimes caused prejudice and conflict, but insofar as they lent cohesion to groups they were the basis for organizing effectively a complex society. They permitted each individual to find an appropriate affiliation, free of interference from others or from the government. Life in the United States, therefore, did not homogenize its people; regional and ethnic variations enabled men and women to preserve their distinctive qualities as human beings. For a long time, furthermore, the relative emptiness of the land minimized friction. Strangers found room either to establish communities of their own or to filter in among the earlier arrivals.

By the middle of the eighteenth century the acceptance of diversity had become an essential ingredient of national character, even before the nation existed as a governmental entity. The American Revolution — which gave official sanction to this acceptance — was a national as well as a social and political movement. It achieved a separation of the colonies from Britain and it also established the basis of the future polity. The Founding Fathers did not make familial descent or place of birth a test of nationality, as in Europe. Instead, they invented a totally new concept, citizenship, which described the actualities of the society already in being. Anyone who wished to participate in the affairs of the republic could be a citizen; and any man free to immigrate could enjoy the advantages of the United States on terms of complete equality with those already there. The contemporaries of Washington and Jefferson had faith that free institutions and open opportunity would convert people of any background into citizens.

The Negro slave was an exception to this formula. In 1776 most Americans hoped that slavery would ultimately disappear; but they could not conceive how a former master and a former bondsman could live together as equals. The failure to agree on a solution to this problem led to decades of conflict that ended in civil war. The Constitution went no further toward solving this problem than to limit the importation of additional slaves. There also were ambiguities in the attitude toward the Indians, who were regarded sometimes as prospects for conversion and civilization, sometimes as noble savages, and sometimes simply as obstacles to the spread of settlement.

Concern about American national character deepened in the second half of the nineteenth century. The sectional crisis and the Civil War revealed the cleavage between North and South, while immigration brought into the country new peoples — Irish Catholics, Polish Jews, Chinese "coolies" — who seemed not to assimilate as readily as their predecessors. Before the century ended, many Americans also were troubled by the position of the freed but still underprivileged Negroes and by the problems of those alien peoples who were subjected to United States imperialism.

Increasingly, those who remained optimistic insisted that the nation was a melting pot which would ultimately create a single stock improved by the diverse ingredients pouring into it. It followed, therefore, that the newcomers must learn the manners, habits, language, and faith of those Americans who had been established in the land for a longer period. The more pessimistic concluded that the task was hopeless, that the dissimilar peoples would never fuse. Newer concepts taught that the differences of race were ineradicable. Therefore, it was believed necessary to subordinate inferior types, such as the Negroes were thought to be, and to exclude all further immigration except that which added strength to the original Anglo-Saxon population.

The conflict between these two extreme points of view persisted into the twentieth century and culminated in the 1920s and 1930s when millions of Americans joined such racist organizations as the Ku Klux Klan and the Silver Shirts. Thereafter, the conflict subsided as experience demonstrated that a successful adjustment was possible. In any case, despite the social tensions created by the commingling of so many peoples, a majority of Americans probably understood all along that diversity was the rule rather than the exception in their society and rejected extremist solutions. As a practical matter, they understood that their neighbors spoke with different accents, worshiped in different churches, belonged to different clubs, and still were good neighbors.

The divisions among its peoples helped shape the free institutions of the United States. Because they were not homogeneous, for example, Americans did not turn to government to supply all their social needs. In many matters they acted cooperatively — rather than through the instruments of force controlled by the state — and the individual could make his own choices. Once different sects appeared, for instance, the law could no longer regulate worship as it had in seventeenth-century New England. By the terms of the Constitution, the government could neither support religion nor regulate it by law. Religious practice depended entirely upon voluntary associations. The consequences of the complete separation of church and state would continue to unfold in the centuries after ratification of the First Amendment, but the basic principle was an actuality even before the First Congress met. As a result the United States escaped the problems which had been responsible for many of the wars in Europe. "This whole vast chapter of debate and strife" remained unopened in the United States, commented Lord Bryce in 1885. All religious bodies were "absolutely equal before the law, and unrecognized by the law, except as voluntary associations of private citizens."

Many features of the economy, of the culture, and of education, philanthropy, and family life were also voluntary. Corporations rather than government agencies generally operated the turnpikes, canals, railroads, and telephone systems. Autonomous groups supported artistic and literary activities. George Washington's vision of a national university came to nothing, but there was no lack of institutions of higher education, private as well as public. Nor did the state secure a monopoly of other schools or of medical or welfare institutions.

The distinctive organization of American society profoundly influenced its culture. Individuals of every background contributed to the scientific, literary, musical, and artistic life of the nation; and the contact of millions of strange men who were forced to live on terms of relative equality with one another had a deep effect upon all of them.

American culture was never subject to strong controls. There was never a single correct way of speaking or a uniform style of writing and research. Harvard did not set standards in the United States as did the Sorbonne in France or Oxford and Cambridge in England. Even in the small closed communities (such as the one Sinclair Lewis described in *Main Street*) where attempts were made to enforce conformity, dissident individuals and groups could go their own way without much interference. Tolerance was even more characteristic of the great cities where residents were shielded by anonymity and of the frontier where greater space enabled each man to establish his own identity.

The efforts made at the end of the nineteenth century to define a genteel tradition in literature, art, and music ended in failure. The metropolitan social elite controlled the prestigious magazines, the opera, and the museums. The excluded groups, however, expressed their own impulses in the realistic novel, in jazz, and in the movies; and their ability to break through artificial limitations gave American culture renewed vitality.

Above all, diversity was itself a source of richness.

American literature was always basically English, not only in its language and style, but also in its continuing responsiveness to literary trends in the former mother country. Nevertheless, American literature was repeatedly invigorated by fresh perceptions of the peculiarities of the society in which it was written. Yankee and southern writers dealt with distinctly different worlds; and the attention to "local color" persisted well beyond 1900. A distinctive western influence animated the work of Bret Harte, Mark Twain, and Hamlin Garland. In the twentieth century, the Negroes and the children of German, Irish, Jewish, and Italian immigrants added to the complexity of the pattern. Sinclair Lewis, Theodore Dreiser, F. Scott Fitzgerald, and Richard Wright used a common language and shared many assumptions; yet the influence of origin was apparent in the writings of each.

Diversity also sustained the freedom and therefore the strength of American religious life. Sectarianism was characteristic. Some denominations, like the German Lutherans, the Greek Orthodox, and the Scotch-Irish Presbyterians, were themselves the products of immigration. Others, such as the Unitarians, arose from schisms that reflected different theological opinions. Still others were the results of the activities of native prophets — for example, the Church of the Latter Day Saints led by Joseph Smith, the Adventists led by William Miller, and the Christian Scientists led by Mary Baker Eddy. Although these were all Protestant churches, each clung to its own doctrines and each usually attracted adherents having common social characteristics.

Catholicism in the United States, like Lutheranism, was a product of immigration. But the Catholic Church was neither monolithic nor detached from American life. On the one hand, the Irish, the Italians, and the Poles retained their own distinctive forms of worship for many years; on the other, the Church quickly accommodated itself to America. It retained its unity but it permitted local parishes to serve the needs of each group it embraced. Furthermore, by ceasing to claim that it offered the sole road to salvation, the Catholic Church adjusted to the conditions of coexistence in a pluralistic society. Consequently, the Church was not simply the arm of a foreign body operating in the United States but an American institution. The Jews, who also transplanted an orthodox faith, likewise adapted their religious ideas and practices to conditions in the United States.

The same environment influenced Americans of every

religious affiliation. Science, the mass media, and public education created similarities in worship, social activities and basic ideas. In all sects the role of the laity expanded; and the insistence upon a unique path to salvation gave way to a tolerant acceptance of differences.

Yet, Americanization did not make all the faiths alike nor destroy their ethnic qualities. The very conditions of coexistence created the assumption that each man, in going to the church of his choice, would probably adhere to the faith of his fathers. Consequently, adjustment to American conditions strengthened religion. There was no organized anticlerical movement as there was in Europe. The completely voluntary nature of worship in the United States encouraged each man to seek God in his own way; and it assured the churches of the loyalty and support of those who chose to join.

The economic and social effects of mobility and diversity were profound. The gigantic task of developing a dynamic economy without curtailing the liberty of the people depended upon the availability of manpower. The initial process of clearing the wilderness required a steady flow of men to the frontier; the construction of towns and of an effective transportation system called for other forms of labor; and industrialization hinged upon the presence of workers to tend the machines. There were enough people glad to take up the axe, the spade, or the hod, as well as others with entrepreneurial and engineering skills so that all the calls for manpower could be filled without compulsion. A static society could not have adjusted to such pressures of economic change.

The intricate group life of the nation prevented the appearance of hard-and-fast class lines. No one was simply a worker, a farmer, or a merchant. Beyond this, each individual had affiliations with an ethnic or regional group; and he was linked through religious and social organizations with men in other occupations. These connections supplied even the depressed elements of the population with a leadership competent to express their grievances. As a result, class consciousness was weakened and some of the bitterness of economic conflict was absorbed. Perhaps that was why the labor movement in the United States never sought to destroy but only to share in the existing social system.

The pluralism of American life also weakened class consciousness by encouraging rapid social mobility. Few men in the nineteenth and twentieth centuries could assume that they would automatically move into their fathers' positions; there was always the danger of a fall, always the possibility of a rise. Although the myth of the self-made man who moved from rags to riches through prudence and hard work was a gross exaggeration, moderate climbs and declines were characteristic.

Expansion, in itself, tended to broaden opportunities. The territorial and industrial frontiers gave ambitious people a chance to make their way, but they also made it hazardous for anyone to depend solely on inherited wealth or status. In addition, migration — whether from abroad, as in the case of Europeans in the 1850s, or internal, as in the case of southern Negroes in the 1950s — tended to place newcomers at the bottom of the social scale and thus raise the social level of those who had arrived earlier. Finally, each ethnic group offered its members some channels for advancement, as it called for services of its own lawyers and shopkeepers and other professionals and businessmen. Only bondage or prejudice could block off access to desirable occupations outside the confines of the ethnic community; consequently the Negroes, who suffered from both, encountered greater difficulty than other Americans in making the most of their abilities. They were in an anomalous situation in a society which, in all other instances, encouraged the pursuit of happiness.

A subtle interplay of social and political forces gave American government its characteristic features. The Founding Fathers derived the basic forms of the state and federal systems from their English heritage and from colonial experience. The authors of the national Constitution and of the state constitutions framed in the decades after independence incorporated into those instruments their beliefs regarding a proper allocation of power to assure both effective administration and freedom for the individual. But the constitutions were living documents, and in the centuries that followed they were transformed by the people who lived under them.

The constitutions, for instance, made no provision for political parties, which were to become vital instruments in the actual operations of government. These organizations, which had taken shape before the end of the eighteenth century, became prominent during the Jacksonian era. The party system mobilized and informed the electorate and offered it a significant choice of alternative candidates and policies. Through the party system also, a federal government of intricate checks and balances was able to make and execute decisions.

In the formation of the party system, regional and ethnic

differences as well as economic interests and intellectual convictions were of great importance. Sectional and ethnic factors were already significant by the time the Democratic-Federalist division appeared; they became even more significant in the Jacksonian era; and they acquired a formal structure in the political machines that had been developed by the end of the nineteenth century.

Two important consequences flowed from these circumstances: American political parties never became monolithic, as did many such parties in the European democracies; and no political organization represented a single class interest or a uniform ideological point of view. The party leader was compelled to reconcile the divergent groupings, the alliance of which supplied him with his support. He could move toward change, but only by the methods of compromise and adjustment. Furthermore, because it had to be responsive to the expressed wishes of its clientele, the party served as a channel of communication between the governed and their government. Party responsibility compelled elected officials, at whatever level, to take account of the needs of the people. Therein the United States differed from most other democracies in which officeholders accounted to the citizens only at elections.

These institutions — the constitutions and the political parties — were the links between the national character of the Americans and the diversity which was the underlying quality of their historic experience. In a great and variegated land settled by men who were strangers to it and to each other, the people, forced to move about constantly, developed a pattern of free political and social institutions that emphasized voluntary action. An expansive economy created opportunities that justified risk-taking; and the absence of external restraints provided emotional latitude for a variety of religious and cultural expressions. These conditions were congenial to the personality types that became defined as American — types characterized by restlessness, by a disregard of status, and by a competitive individualism that could be harnessed to great tasks more readily by methods of cooperation than by those of constraint.

Oscar Handlin, Director
Charles Warren Center for Studies in American History
Harvard University

This New Man

A Discourse in Portraits

The American Is . . .

. . . Restless and Mobile

Impatient, dissatisfied, seeking ever more elbow room for himself, his ambitions, and his ideas, the American is a nomad. Discontent — with established restrictions and closed opportunities — drove him to strange, forbidding shores. And discontent drove him to push this new frontier of the original colonies farther and farther back — to the Pacific shelf, and beyond. With the vanishing of territorial frontiers the same restless urge has led him into other unexplored terrains: the depths of the earth and ocean, the psyche and collective unconscious, molecular and atomic energy, electronics and outer space. If asked to explain his compulsive mobility, to state what he is seeking, he will seldom give the same answer: Freedom. Room. A better living. Adventure. Success. Satisfaction of curiosity. Love of competition. Better opportunities for his children. Fulfillment. Often he has no answer at all.

But he has kept on moving: from place to place; from east to west, and south to north; from farm to city; from redbrick schoolhouse to university; from poverty to wealth, if he is able and lucky. Because change has so often been for the better, he has come to regard it as an absolute good. Translated into a metaphor for social justice and economic opportunity, the "New Frontier" can still rally Americans to strive for a larger future. With a self-confidence non-Americans find naive but impressive, each new generation has believed of itself what Thomas Paine proclaimed for the men of the Revolution:

We have it in our power to begin the world over again. A situation similar to the present has not happened since the days of Noah. The birthday of a new world is at hand.

24

Explorers

The challenge of uncharted seas and unmapped lands originally brought Western Europeans to America and left later Americans unsatisfied until a whole new continent lay revealed before them. Spanish conquistadors, laboring for "God, gold, and glory," pushed through the marshes and uplands of the South or across the deserts and valleys of the Southwest, while Jesuit priests and obscure fur trappers paddled down the great river and lake systems of the North to build altars and trading posts in the forest. The English explored more slowly and settled as they went westward from the Atlantic, duplicating the homes and towns they had left behind. Throughout the nineteenth century the later explorers blazed trails across the Rockies and the high plains to the Pacific.

Intent upon exploiting the inexhaustible resources of their own country, Americans for a long time left the exploration of other continents to Europeans. Only in the last century have they begun to turn their attention to new worlds — beyond the limits of territorial space. The occasional theoretical physicist or cosmographer was a lonely figure until newly arrived Americans like Einstein and Enrico Fermi, fleeing the fascist tyranny of the 1930s, opened American eyes to worlds of limitless space.

WILLIAM CLARK *Frontier Geographer* **1770-1838**

Long after the return of the Lewis and Clark expedition of 1804-1806, the memory of the "Red-Headed Chief," William Clark, lived on among the Indians of the Northern Plains and the far Northwest. Clark's experience on the frontier and his intuitive sense of geography made him an ideal coleader of the great venture to solve the riddle of the Northwest Passage.

An Indian fighter from youth, Clark was educated in the ways of the wilderness. His older brother, the frontier hero George Rogers Clark, had once been approached by Thomas Jefferson to explore the far Northwest. Meriwether Lewis' invitation to the younger Clark to join him in an overland expedition to the Pacific fulfilled a family destiny and was eagerly

accepted. In vigorous, unsophisticated prose, Clark's notes and diaries record the difficult trip from St. Louis across the Great Divide and down the Columbia River to its mouth. At its conclusion he wrote triumphantly, "Ocian in view! O! the joy." An accomplished cartographer and draftsman, his maps and his sketches of birds, fish, and wild animals did much to document the expedition.

Following the expedition Clark settled at St. Louis. Governor of the Missouri Territory during the War of 1812 and superintendent of Indian affairs until his death, he was largely responsible for frontier defenses against the Indians and for the peaceful reconciliation that followed.

JOHN WESLEY JARVIS, oil on canvas, 30 x 35, not dated
Lent by Missouri Historical Society, St. Louis, Missouri

NATHANIEL BOWDITCH *Practical Navigator* 1773-1838

A ship chandler's apprentice of Salem with some local reputation for mathematics, Nathaniel Bowditch was plunged into fame at the age of twenty-six. In 1799 a Massachusetts printer, bent on a rather ordinary piracy, commissioned Bowditch to make the revisions for an American edition of a popular English nautical manual. The young mariner eliminated so many errors that the new edition largely superseded the original work in England as well as America. In 1802 a third edition, titled *The New American Practical Navigator*, boldly announced Nathaniel Bowditch as its sole author. Although revised by many editors since the United States Government purchased the copyright in 1867, it is still known in marine libraries as *Bowditch*.

Nathaniel Bowditch was no stranger to navigation. He made five voyages to every quarter of the globe between 1795 and 1804. Meanwhile he studied French,

Italian, German, Spanish, Greek, and — in order to read Newton's *Principia* — Latin. His capacity for methodical concentration became legendary. Sailors spread the yarn that during a sea fight with a privateer the gunners found Bowditch sitting on a keg of powder and working out a mathematical problem on his slate.

Although he had left school at the age of ten, Bowditch collected numerous honorary degrees, belonged to many learned societies, and served as an overseer of Harvard University. He became the president of one insurance company and an actuary for another, but his first loves were astronomy and mathematics. His scientific reputation rests chiefly on his English translation, with extensive commentary, of the *Méca-nique Céleste* by the Marquis de Laplace, whose marble bust can be seen in the upper left corner of this portrait.

CHARLES OSGOOD, oil on canvas, 58 x 43½, 1835
Lent by Peabody Museum, Salem, Massachusetts

MERIWETHER LEWIS *Inland Voyager*

1774-1809

As the official commander of the United States expedition to the far Northwest (1804-1806), Captain Meriwether Lewis explored the unknown and often fantasized lands of the upper Missouri River, Rocky Mountains, and the Northwest. The expedition opened the region to fur traders and in time to settlers, while it reinforced the nation's claim to the Oregon country.

Lewis, born into a well-to-do family near Charlottesville, Virginia, was schooled as a boy in mathematics and elementary science. In 1795 he joined the United States Army as an ensign, serving on the Ohio Valley frontier until 1801 when he became private secretary

to his Virginia neighbor and the newly elected President, Thomas Jefferson. Among the projects frequently discussed by the President's inner circle was exploration for a land route to the Pacific. In selecting Lewis to head such an expedition, Jefferson picked an experienced man of known intelligence, daring, and determination — qualities that proved to be much needed on the two-and-a-half-year trek from St. Louis to the mouth of the Columbia River and back.

Following his successful exploration Lewis served successfully as governor of the Louisiana Territory until his death — by murder or suicide — in 1809.

CHARLES BALTHAZAR JULIEN FEORET DE SAINT-MÉMIN, chalk on pink paper, 20½ x 13½, not dated
Lent by Missouri Historical Society, St. Louis, Missouri

CHARLES WILKES   *Polar Scientist*   **1798-1877**

America's interest in Antarctica began with the expedition, from 1838 to 1842, led by the frustrated and long-unappreciated Charles Wilkes. The voyage first demonstrated that Antarctica was a continent, an achievement commemorated by that part of the south polar continent named Wilkes Land.

Born in New York City, Wilkes went to sea at seventeen, serving first in the merchant marine and then in the United States Navy. Eventually he was made head of the Depot of Charts and Instruments in Washington, D. C. In 1838, as a lieutenant, he was given command of a flagship and five other vessels to explore the Pacific coasts of America, the South Seas, and Antarctica. Poorly equipped for polar exploration and

troubled by friction and desertions, the expedition was nonetheless a scientific success. For Wilkes, however, it brought personal disappointments. On his return in 1842 he was court-martialed for his treatment of seamen, and his discoveries were long contested by European explorers.

During the Civil War Wilkes achieved fleeting national fame when he seized the Confederate diplomatic commissioners James M. Mason and John Slidell from the British ship *Trent*, precipitating the "Trent Affair," a dangerous diplomatic incident. Wilkes retired in 1866, having been commissioned a rear admiral.

SAMUEL B. WAUGH, oil on canvas, 24 x 20, 1870
NPG. 67.63

ROBERT MILLIKAN *Public-Spirited Physicist* **1868-1953**

In 1893 Robert Millikan, a minister's son from Iowa and onetime physical education instructor, decided in earnest to become a physicist. At that time America was only dimly aware of having a scientific future. After two years as Columbia University's only graduate student in physics, Millikan went to Germany for further study with some of the best scientists of the late years of the nineteenth century.

Through his contributions both to pure science and the establishment of graduate centers, this pioneering physicist played a large role in bringing America to scientific hegemony. In 1923 Millikan was awarded the Nobel Prize for his work on the photoelectric effect and on isolating the electron and measuring its electric charge. He wrote pioneering textbooks, served on

the organizing committee of the National Research Council, and directed the Norman Bridge Laboratory of Physics at the California Institute of Technology for nearly twenty-five years.

Throughout his career Millikan was influential in making the results of pure science available to industry and government. During World War II he was instrumental in mobilizing America's scientific resources to advance the war effort. A religious as well as a scientific man, he at the same time had doubts about the future: "Unless by our joint efforts we do find a way specifically to put an end to world wars and their mass killings, the human race has the possibility, indeed the likelihood, of destroying itself."

HOLGER AND HELEN W. JENSEN, bronze, 24 high, 1942
Lent by California Institute of Technology

ALBERT EINSTEIN *Earth Shaker*   **1879-1955**

When Nobel Prize winner Albert Einstein left his native Germany in 1933 — fleeing a Nazi takeover — and emigrated to the United States he was already the most famous scientist in the world. His special theory of relativity, published in 1905 when he was twenty-six, and the general theory of a decade later constituted the first major revisions of the static Newtonian universe. With these theories modern man was obliged to revisualize the known world. Ironically, the explorations of this gentle man blossomed in destructive violence. When the uranium atom was split in 1939, the nuclear energy released was measured by using Einstein's equation $E = mc^2$.

Einstein influenced the American atomic bomb effort in still another way. In 1939 he wrote directly to President Franklin Roosevelt to warn that a bomb of great destructiveness was conceivable as a result of recent research in nuclear physics. Germany, Einstein warned, might have begun already to develop such a weapon. His letter contributed to the sense of urgency which led to the Manhattan Project and the first atomic bomb.

This portrait of Einstein was painted from life in 1950 by Josef Scharl (1864-1954), a long-time friend and fellow fugitive from Hitler's Germany. It evokes memories of the familiar figure in baggy trousers, old sweater, and black knitted cap shuffling about the grounds of the Institute for Advanced Study at Princeton, New Jersey.

JOSEF SCHARL, oil on canvas, 35¼ x 28¼, 1950
NPG. 66.6

ROBERT HUTCHINS GODDARD *Rocketeer*   **1882-1945**

A matter-of-fact, diminutive New Englander, Robert Hutchins Goddard became a pioneer in American rocket research. Beginning his investigations in 1909 at Clark University, he persevered through years of professional neglect and financial failure. The press delighted in ridiculing him when his rockets soared to 61 feet, falling 200,000 miles short of the moon, at which they were directed. And his neighbors, alarmed by his experiments in the quiet Massachusetts countryside, demanded anti-rocket legislation.

During the 1930s, with support from the Daniel and Florence Guggenheim Foundation, Goddard carried on his work at an isolated site near Roswell, New Mexico.

Meanwhile he enviously watched German engineers develop a rocket program with resources far beyond his own means. But to him belongs the credit for working out the fundamental theory of jet propulsion and rocket flight. "Dr. Goddard," observed Wernher von Braun, "was ahead of us all."

This pioneer, however, did not live to see the massive multibillion-dollar space program which he more than any other man had made possible. The Goddard Space Flight Center at Greenbelt, Maryland, commemorates the courageous scientist once mocked as the "moon-rocket man."

EMILY BURLING WAITE, oil on canvas, 28 x 24, not dated
Gift of an anonymous donor NPG.68.3

Frontiersmen and Expansionists

Americans are always moving on.
It's an old Spanish custom gone astray,
A sort of English fever, I believe,
Or just a mere desire to take French leave,
I couldn't say. I couldn't really say.
But, when the whistle blows, they go away.
Sometimes there never was a whistle blown,
But they don't care, for they can blow their own
Whistles of willow-stick and rabbit-bone,
Quail-calling through the rain
A dozen tunes but only one refrain,
"We don't know where we're going, but we're on our way!"
— Bird-whistles, sleepy with Virginia night,
Veery and oriole,
Calling the morning from the Chesapeake
To rise, in pomp, with redbud at her breast,
The whistles of the great trains going west,
Lonely, at night, through cold Nebraska towns,
The chunking of the bullfrogs in the creek
Where the forgotten wampum slowly drowns,
Cow-horn and turkey-call,
And last, purest of all,
The spell of peace, the rapture of the ear,
The water-music mounting into light,
The hermit thrush that is New England's soul —
These are the notes they hear.
    *   *   *   *   *
Oh, paint your wagons with "Pike's Peak or Bust!"
Pack up the fiddle, rosin up the bow,
Vamoose, skedaddle, mosey, hit the grit!
(We pick our words, like nuggets, for the shine,
And, where they didn't fit, we make them fit,
Whittling a language out of birch and pine.)
We're off for Californ-iay,
We're off down the wild O-hi-o!
And every girl on Natchez bluff
Will cry as we go by-o!
    *   *   *   *   *
So, when the gospel train pulls out
And God calls "All aboard!"
Will you be there with the Lord, brother,
Will you be there with the Lord?
Yes, I'll be there,
Oh, I'll be there,
I'll have crossed that rolling river in the morning!

Stephen Vincent Benét,
from *Western Star*

DANIEL BOONE   *Frontier Legend*   **1734-1820**

In 1775 Daniel Boone and his party pressed through the Cumberland Gap to the fertile bluegrass lands west of the mountains. There they established Boonesborough on the Kentucky River, leaving behind them the Wilderness Road as a route for settlers to follow. Boone was not the first man to penetrate the mountains, nor even the first to attempt settlement there. But it was his adventures in that "dark and bloody ground" that breached the psychological barrier of the Appalachians. Kentucky was quickly settled, and the American West, at least as far as the Mississippi, opened to waves of migrants.

Boone the man and Boone the legend became inseparable. His solitary treks in search of furs, battles with the fierce Shawnees, and remarkable skill in finding his way through trackless wilds were well known even before 1775. Although never lost, he admitted that he was once "bewildered for three days."

In his later years, when he had moved farther west to wander the country beyond the Mississippi, he became what he has always remained, the archetype of the frontier hero. Lord Byron celebrated him in verse as a "child of Nature," living in the lonely but happy world beyond civilization. And James Fenimore Cooper used him as a model for his wilderness hero, Natty Bumppo. Although many of the accomplishments with which he was credited were apocryphal, Daniel Boone embodied the finest qualities of the frontier: fearlessness, stamina, expertness in woodcraft and riflery, and the cavalier ethic.

CHESTER HARDING, oil on canvas, 21½ x 16½, possibly 1820
Lent by Massachusetts Historical Society, Boston, Massachusetts

BLAKESLEE-LANE, INC., BALTIMORE

FRANCIS ASBURY *Bishop on Horseback*   **1745-1816**

To Francis Asbury, Methodist missionary and first Methodist bishop in America, the frontier wilderness was a battleground in a war of a different kind. The prize was souls, not land. During the forty-five years after he landed at Philadelphia, Asbury traveled over a quarter of a million miles by foot, horseback, and carriage, carrying the message of spiritual and moral regeneration. His address, he told an English friend, was simply "America" — any postmaster would know him and hold his mail.

Like many early Methodists, Asbury came from the humble, hard-working folk of England to whom John Wesley preached. Born near Birmingham and converted in his teens, he served an apprenticeship as a circuit preacher before coming to the New World in 1771. In America, and especially on the sparsely settled frontier, the Wesleyan call to individual religious renewal and righteous conduct was enthusiastically received. Asbury's own achievement, however, lay less in his preaching than in his leadership and organizational ability. He steered the infant church through the critical years of the American Revolution when its existence was threatened by divided loyalties. Outmaneuvering even the forceful Wesley and appointing himself bishop, he assumed virtual control of the entire Methodist organization in this country.

At Asbury's urging the Methodists became in 1789 the first religious group to accept the Government of the United States. His hundreds of circuit riders, carrying the Christian message in their saddlebags, and his innumerable local preachers, Sunday schools, and pioneer publishing enterprises planted Methodism permanently in the life of the new nation.

CHARLES PEALE POLK, oil on canvas, 37¾ x 31⅝, 1794
Lent by Methodist Historical Society, Lovely Lane Museum, Baltimore

SAM HOUSTON *Border Chief*   **1793-1863**

As a boy Sam Houston left home to live with the Cherokee Indians. Adopted later under the tribal name "The Raven," symbolizing good fortune, he was a lifelong friend of red men and a defender of their interests.

Houston's courage, ability to command, sense of honor, and tall, manly frame made him a leader on the frontier. A flamboyant personality and a passionate attachment to certain causes attracted many devoted friends — ranging from Indian chiefs to Andrew Jackson — but also made him a target for attacks by enemies. After many turbulent years, however, his passions eventually cooled.

While still a young man, Houston became a Congressman and then Governor of Tennessee. When the failure of his first marriage destroyed his political career he returned to his first friends, the Indians, and served as their representative on missions to Washington. After an interval of drink and despondency he set out to make a new life as a land speculator and opportunist in Texas. Arriving early in the war for Texan independence, he helped establish Texas as the new Lone Star Republic and became its president. He was successively United States Senator and Governor of Texas, following annexation.

Upon the secession of Texas from the Union in 1861 Houston refused to take an oath of allegiance to the Confederacy on the ground that Texas had returned to its status as an independent republic. When he was accordingly deposed, he declined the offer of Union soldiers to reinstate him for fear of subjecting his beloved state to further conflict.

HENRY DEXTER, plaster, 23½ high, 1860
Lent by Texas Library and Historical Commission, Texas State Library, Austin, Texas

北亞墨利加人物

ペルリ像

MATTHEW C. PERRY *Yankee in Nippon* **1794-1858**

Commodore Matthew C. Perry's voyages of 1853 and 1864 opened Japan to American trade and Western influence. The arrival of the Americans had a great impact on the Japanese, who had seen few Westerners before Perry's expedition. Court painters, as well as artists for popular news sheets, flocked to the ships to depict the historic event and to satisfy the public's curiosity about the barbarians. A popular subject, Perry was portrayed in many moods. In this woodblock print inscribed "Portrait of Peruri, a North American," he is stern and forbidding.

The intelligence, forcefulness, and tact which stood Perry well in his negotiations with the reluctant Japanese had made him a good naval officer as well. "Old Bruin," as he was known to his men, helped establish the steam navy and the Naval Academy at Annapolis. During the Mexican War, he had commanded the Gulf Squadron in the blockade and seizure of Vera Cruz. But most important, he was one of the first Americans to anticipate the crucial role of the Pacific in the United States' development as a world power.

UNIDENTIFIED JAPANESE ARTIST, color woodcut on paper, 14¾ x 10, not dated
Lent by the Library of Congress

WILLIAM H. SEWARD   *Political Expansionist*   **1801-1872**

A native of New York State who became first its Governor and then United States Senator, William H. Seward was as interested in pushing back American frontiers as the hardiest traveler on the Oregon Trail. His two terms as Senator (1849-1861) and his appointment as Secretary of State under Presidents Abraham Lincoln and Andrew Johnson gave him ample opportunity to do something about it.

In the Senate his main concern was to stop the spread of slavery to the West, where he feared it would discourage small farmers from settling territory already belonging to the United States. Furthermore, he cast a covetous eye on lands which might be acquired in the future. Campaigning for Lincoln in 1860, he told the people of St. Paul, Minnesota, that Canada would one day be a part of the United States with the national capital located near the headwaters of the Mississippi River. In 1867 he attempted to make good this grandiose promise when he negotiated the purchase of Alaska.

FRANK BUCHSER, oil on canvas, 54 x 40¼, not dated
Lent by Kunstmuseum, Basel, Switzerland

BRIGHAM YOUNG *American Moses*   **1801-1877**

In the summer of 1847 a group of covered wagons carrying Latter Day Saints into the wilderness arrived in the Great Salt Lake Basin. These people were the vanguard of a great exodus of Mormons led purposely by Brigham Young into a barren and uninviting promised land. Here, in a region that no other settlers would want, they hoped to find peace at last. By 1869 about 80,000 Mormons from all over the world had crossed the desert, many of them pushing their possessions in handcarts.

Young, the president of the Church, was made governor of the Mexican State of Deseret, in which the settlement was located, and later of the American Ter-

ritory of Utah. Under his leadership the Latter Day Saints pioneered in irrigation and founded schools, tabernacles, and theaters. He established good relations with nearby Indians on the eminently practical theory that it was better to feed them than to fight them. To young Mormons made restless by tales of California gold fields he said, "Go and be damned." Most of them stayed.

A frontiersman by birth — in backwoods Vermont — and by choice when he led the Mormons westward, Young had the same gift for organization which built industries and made fortunes for other men. Instead, he defended a faith and peopled a wilderness.

Hartwig Bornemann, lithograph on paper, 30 x 25, not dated
Gift of The Church of Jesus Christ of Latter Day Saints   *NPG. 67.57*

JOHN A. SUTTER *California Colonizer* 1803-1880

On 24 January 1848 gold was discovered in the Sacramento Valley near the large Mexican land grant of "General" John A. Sutter, a Swiss immigrant. Sutter immediately leased the gold-bearing land from its Indian owners but it proved a curse rather than a blessing. The ensuing gold rush, which populated California so quickly that it became a state in 1850, left Sutter with his livestock scattered, his ranch hands lured elsewhere, and his wheatfields occupied by squatters. What had been a private empire named Nueva Helvetia, with its own factories, smithies, distillery, and cooperage, became first a ghost settlement and then a boom town completely overrun by prospec-

tors and other adventurers. Sutter himself, a generous, hospitable adventurer and a smooth, crafty opportunist by turns, entered a long decline. Thirty-two years after the historic discovery at "Sutter's Mill," the bankrupt victim died in Washington, D. C., where he had made vain efforts to obtain from Congress compensation for his losses.

Ironically, Sutter, who had founded his own principality, contributed significantly to the bridging of the eastern and western United States. After 1850 the frontier moved eastward from California as well as westward from the Mississippi.

FRANK BUCHSER, oil on canvas, 27½ x 21½, 1866
Lent by Museum der Stadt Solothurn, Solothurn, Switzerland

JOHN CHARLES FRÉMONT *Luckless Trailblazer*   **1813-1890**

To thousands of settlers moving west in the middle years of the nineteenth century, John Charles Frémont was the "Pathfinder," the man who had blazed wagon trails through the mountains to the rich lands of the Pacific coast. History has dimmed his romantic reputation, for most if not all the paths were already known to the trail-wise mountain men like Kit Carson and "Old Bill" Williams who accompanied him. But the detailed maps and vivid reports of Frémont's four western expeditions between 1842 and 1853 demonstrated the feasibility of overland travel to the Far West, luring restless men to make the great trek.

As befits a hero of romance, Frémont was pursued by a nemesis which turned his successes into failures. In 1846 he played an important role in the forcible annexation of California, only to be court-martialed for insubordination. The gold found on his huge Mariposa estate slipped through his fingers. He was defeated as the new Republican Party's first presidential candidate in 1856. Finally, his extravagance and arbitrary handling of confiscated property led Lincoln to remove him as commanding general at St. Louis during the Civil War.

CHARLES LORING ELLIOTT, oil on canvas, 35 x 28½, not dated
Lent by The Brooklyn Museum, Brooklyn, New York

Immigrants
and
Expatriates

Abundant land and land of abundance — two keys to American history. For nearly three centuries immigrants from all parts of the world poured in a steady stream into the great port cities of the Atlantic and Pacific coasts. At first they came to possess the land itself. To own a plot of ground and do with it as one pleased was not even a dream for the majority of Europeans. Those who arrived later came to fill jobs created by the land and its products. There were forests to clear; canals, railroads, and highways to build; rich veins to mine; and machinery to be run. All that was needed was a good strong back and the will to succeed.

And so the "rising men" of the Old World peopled the New. Except for the slaves, tragically involuntary immigrants, the newcomers were neither the hopeless nor the self-satisfied, but the confident and adventurous. Into the melting pot went English, Scotch, Irish, Germans, French, Spaniards, Scandinavians, Slavs, Southern Europeans, and Asiatics; in less than a generation out came Americans — unlike any other nationality but bearing a mystic kinship to all.

Materialism, which was always a strong motivation in those who came to America, in time became insufferable to many whose roots were deepest. While a tide of humanity flowed onto American shores from abroad, an undertow of expatriates in search of cultural or spiritual fulfillment began to wash back to the Old World. At the same time, organized labor, which feared cheap competition, and racists, who feared contamination, joined forces in an effort to shut America's portals against further mass immigration. Today the huge immigrant receiving station at Ellis Island is closed. But American character is richer and more vital because of its heterogeneous heritage.

RICHARD LEE   *English Squire in Virginia*   **1613?-1664**

Richard Lee, the first of the famous Lees of Virginia, arrived in York County about 1641. He brought with him a large number of indentured servants, for each of whom he was granted fifty acres of land. Unlike the later immigrant of peasant background who could only hope that his children or grandchildren might achieve prominence, Lee soon became a member of the House of Burgesses and of the Governor's Council; he also served as Secretary of State in the colony. His profits as leading landowner, merchant, and ship-owner made him one of the wealthiest men in Virginia.

Although he continued to live in Virginia, Lee remained the English gentleman. When he visited London in 1661 he considered remaining permanently in England, where an absentee squire and merchant could protect his colonial interests as well as in Virginia. Times had changed by July 1776 when two of his descendants, Richard Henry Lee and Francis Lightfoot Lee, signed the Declaration of Independence.

Attributed to Sir Peter Lely, oil on canvas, 30 x 24¾, possibly 1661 or 1662
Lent by Mrs. Cazenove Lee

JOSEPH PRIESTLEY *Polymath*   **1733-1804**

When Joseph Priestley emigrated to the United States in 1794 his greatest scientific work was behind him. His notable achievements had included the isolation of oxygen, which Lavoisier confirmed and used to lay the foundations of modern chemistry. He had also conducted major experiments in electricity and discovered ammonia and carbon dioxide, among other gases. In leaving behind a secure place in the intellectual life of metropolitan England for the freedom of provincial America, however, he knew what he was about.

Priestley was an early representative of an honorable line — the scientist who has sought out America because his political or religious views were unwelcome in his native land. A republican and utilitarian, Priestley had been burned out of his Birmingham home after his outspoken defense of the French Revolution.

Priestley's free, inquiring intellect carried him into many areas — theology, modern history, and education as well as politics and natural philosophy. Peale's portrait suggests the vitality and strength of this versatile savant who discovered a cure for scurvy, engaged the great Edmund Burke in dramatic debate, helped Thomas Jefferson found the University of Virginia, defended phlogistic chemistry against Lavoisier, and traded blows with the orthodox who disliked his unitarianism and dissenting views.

REMBRANDT PEALE, oil on canvas, 21½ x 18½, not dated
Lent by The New-York Historical Society, New York, New York

JOHN SINGLETON COPLEY *Ill-Fated Exile* **1738-1815**

John Singleton Copley, one of the first native-born painters in America, possessed an intense passion for art but found little to inspire him in his surroundings and no great artists under whom to study. His mother's marriage to the Boston engraver Peter Pelham, however, thrust him into direct contact with engravings of Old World masterpieces. Obtaining what instruction he could from Pelham and others, but largely self-taught, he embarked at fourteen upon the lucrative profession of portrait painting. His ability as a great realist to capture a likeness and to reveal character carried him quickly to the zenith of his American career.

In 1774 Copley left for England, dissatisfied with the limited opportunities of the colonies and disturbed by the revolutionary unrest in Boston. Beginning in London a second career largely as a painter of correctly documented historical scenes, his success mounted until he put off forever plans of returning to America. But in his last years he was inclined to brooding and self-pity when he failed to secure the peace of mind and honors he deserved. His talent gradually deteriorated, critics turned against him, and his paintings were unsold. He died in London, a disillusioned and disgruntled expatriate. Although critics still argue whether he was better as a portrait artist in Boston or as a history painter in London, his success in both genres bears evidence of his exceptional artistic power.

SELF-PORTRAIT, oil on canvas, 18½ in diameter, not dated
Lent by a private collection

ALEXANDER HAMILTON *Enfant Terrible*   1755?-1804

Alexander Hamilton arrived in New York from the Virgin Islands in 1772 as a short, dapper teen-ager. He soon threw himself into the pamphlet war over British taxation, displaying an encyclopedic knowledge of British government and an astonishing ability for incisive reasoning. He served as Washington's aide-de-camp during the Revolution and commanded a regiment at Yorktown. After service in the Confederation Congress and the Constitutional Convention, his eloquent defense of the Constitution in more than half of the *Federalist Papers* contributed to its ratification by New York. He became, at thirty-five, the nation's first Secretary of the Treasury.

In spite of a meteoric career climaxed by his role as virtually Washington's "prime minister," Hamilton was curiously distrustful of democracy. He thought the country should be governed by the "rich and well born," although he was neither. The brilliant young Federalist called for central government to play an active part in shaping the national economy, a radical viewpoint not fully adopted until the administration of Franklin D. Roosevelt. Foreseeing that the United States would grow into a great industrial nation, he sought legislation to hasten the process. His quick, logical intellect and caustic humor made for him a number of enemies. He was killed in a duel with Aaron Burr, whose candidacy for the governorship of New York he had actively opposed.

GIUSEPPE CERACCHI, marble, 23 high, not dated
NPG. 66.30

ALBERT GALLATIN *Economist of Principle*   **1761-1849**

Albert Gallatin arrived in Massachusetts while the colonies were still engaged in the Revolutionary War, but he did not join that struggle. As a young Genevan disciple of Jean Jacques Rousseau, he came to the new republic to exchange the aristocratic traditions of Europe for a simple, primitive life. Accordingly, he first settled in the wilderness of western Pennsylvania.

Gallatin's education and sensitivity to the needs of the frontier made him stand out as a leader of local backwoods democracy. In 1793 he was elected to the United States Senate from Pennsylvania but for political reasons he was denied the seat on the ground that he had not been a citizen for the required nine years. During the Whiskey Rebellion of 1794, the first armed revolt against the authority of the federal gov-

ernment, he persuaded many of the rebels to submit; he was repaid for his loyalty by election to the House of Representatives. His extraordinary grasp of national problems and public finance led him to create the powerful House Ways and Means Committee.

A believer in sound finance and national economic growth, Gallatin became the "laboring oar" of Jefferson's cabinet as Secretary of the Treasury from 1801 to 1811. His tact and intelligence as a diplomat helped President Madison conclude the War of 1812 and maintain peace with France and Canada. After forty years of public service he retired to enter the New York banking community. His pioneering observations of American Indian tribes earned him the title of "father of American ethnology."

GILBERT STUART, oil on canvas, 29⅜ x 23⅞, about 1803
Lent by The Metropolitan Museum of Art, Gift of Frederic W. Stevens, 1908

AUGUST BELMONT *Grateful Capitalist*   **1816-1890**

Born into a wealthy family in Alzei, in the Rhenish Palatinate, August Belmont had little difficulty in establishing a connection with the prominent European banking house of Rothschild. His industry and talent for finance were rewarded by rapid promotion. When a business trip to Cuba coincided with the financial panic of 1837 in the United States, he quickly sensed the possibility of making good out of bad times. He arrived in New York where with almost no capital he rented an office on Wall Street and set up the foundation for his great banking house, August Belmont and Company, the only agent of the Rothschilds in the United States. His success was immediate.

After establishing himself soundly in business, Belmont became an American citizen and married a daughter of Matthew C. Perry. He once said, "I prefer to leave to my children, instead of the gilded prospect of the New York merchant princes, the more enviable title of American citizen . . . ." His position and wealth enabled him to indulge a keen interest in politics and to wield great influence in the Democratic Party. President Franklin Pierce rewarded him for his support by appointing him minister to the Netherlands (1853-1857), a post he filled ably. During the Civil War his devotion to the Union prompted him to help supply troops, raise German volunteers, and act as emissary to European governments. A connoisseur of horses, he served as president of the American Jockey Club and gave his name to Belmont Park, one of the great racetracks of America.

UNIDENTIFIED ARTIST, oil on canvas, 30 x 25, not dated
Lent by August Belmont

CARL SCHURZ *Transplanted Idealist*   **1829-1906**

Throughout his long, varied career Carl Schurz was a "political idealist with the passion of a crusader." A courageous leader in the German revolution of 1848-1849, he was exiled from his homeland as an officer in the revolutionary army, and he was expelled from France as a dangerous foreigner. In America he found a hero's welcome among the German-American population. He wholeheartedly espoused the Negro cause, campaigned for Lincoln, and led a group of German volunteers in the Civil War.

Schurz was the first German-born member of the United States Senate, where, as an uncompromising liberal reformer, he represented Missouri from 1869 to 1875. He attacked the spoils system in the Grant government and public corruption. The Fifteenth Amendment, providing for Negro suffrage, was drafted at his suggestion. As Secretary of the Interior under Rutherford B. Hayes he used his department to test the merit system for civil service, which he advocated for permanent adoption. He held no political office after 1881 but he continued to exert political influence as editor of the New York *Evening Post*, the *Nation*, and *Harper's Weekly*.

ARTHUR VON FERRARIS, oil on canvas, 25¾ x 19½, 1900
Lent by the National Carl Schurz Association, Incorporated, Philadelphia, Pennsylvania

JAMES ABBOTT McNEILL WHISTLER *Barbed Butterfly* **1834-1903**

James A. M. Whistler recognized no country other than the cosmopolitan world of art for art's sake. Denying his Massachusetts birthplace, he said, "I shall be born when and where I want, and I do not choose to be born at Lowell." At the age of twenty-one he set out for Europe to study art, remaining there as the first in the wave of cultural expatriates at the end of the last century. More at home with fellow artists and cosmopolites, he never returned. He was a self-conscious aesthete and dandy, proud of the white lock in his blue-black hair and never appearing without his walking stick. Although he kept the public at a distance with a barbed wit and affectation of conceit, he was intensely conscientious in his work.

Whistler, for whom painting was the "poetry of sight" as music was the "poetry of sound," once said that "the subject-matter has nothing to do with harmony of sound or of color." Calling his works "symphonies," "nocturnes," and "arrangements," he sought a new impersonality and abstraction in art. He incorporated elements of the exquisite and exotic in refining his style, with Spanish and Japanese art having particular influence on him. He was supreme at capturing moods, impressions, and patterns in monochromatic or contrasting color. Long neglected in his native America and scorned by the conventional Britisher in his adopted country, Whistler oscillated between the art capitals of London and Paris where he was lionized.

WILLIAM MERRITT CHASE, oil on canvas, 74⅜ x 36¼, 1885
Lent by The Metropolitan Museum of Art, Bequest of William H. Walker, 1918

THEODORE THOMAS *Musical Tastemaker*   **1835-1905**

Before Theodore Thomas made his influence felt, Americans of his era were inclined to judge the quality of musical performances by their loudness and accompanying showmanship. The principal musical event in Boston in 1869 was an orchestra of 1,000 pieces and a chorus of 10,000 voices rendering martial airs punctuated by cannon shots, which the conductor fired electrically from his desk. Music composed by Americans had little chance of performance.

Thomas emigrated with his family from Germany when he was ten. A pupil of his father and already a well-trained violinist, he helped support the family by playing at dances and weddings and in theaters and saloons. Thomas began to build his own orchestra when he was twenty-seven. To keep his musicians employed full time he took his orchestra to small towns and cities, performing before audiences who talked,

laughed, and made the musicians targets for streams of well-aimed tobacco juice. His programs at first consisted of songs and light waltzes; he then began introducing more classical works and movements from symphonies until he gradually coaxed untutored ears to recognize the beauty of "serious" music.

As conductor of the New York Philharmonic and other orchestras Thomas constantly struggled with patrons who would withdraw support when a season ended in the red. In 1891 a citizens' committee in Chicago organized an orchestra especially for Thomas and guaranteed continued support, regardless of box office receipts. Thomas was finally able to build a great orchestra and to give many American compositions their first hearing. It was thus a German immigrant who began to wean music in America from dependence on European performers and composers.

LEOPOLD SEYFFERT, oil on canvas, 56 x 40, not dated
Lent by The Orchestral Association, Chicago, Illinois, Gift in memory of Oliver W. Norton

HENRY JAMES   *Spectator of the World*   **1843-1916**

Henry James was torn between the personal and cultural claims of two continents. America, where he felt unable to live, claimed his first allegiance as his native country and spiritual refuge. Europe freed him to write and gave him an intricate human scene to observe. An American, he once complained, had to deal "more or less, even if by implication, with Europe; whereas no European is obliged to deal in the least with America." As the principal spokesman for Americans abroad, who found themselves in subtle moral relationships with a society more complex than their own, James recorded the new international scene of leisure and fashion which spread from New York to London, Paris, and Rome.

As a child, he was the victim of his father's enlight-ened theory of education. To make them true cosmopolitans, the elder James moved his children back and forth between the two continents until Henry acquired a sense of rootlessness and a haphazard education. Owing perhaps to a physical infirmity, he never married but lived alone in London or the English countryside. In life as in his psychological novels he adopted an air of complete detachment. Eventually his art became all-important. By perfecting the craft of novel-making, he had a vast influence on authors on both sides of the Atlantic. His best and most disciplined novels, *The Golden Bowl, The Wings of the Dove,* and *The Ambassadors,* were written in these mature years. When his adopted country, England, entered the first World War, he became a British citizen.

JACQUES EMILE BLANCHE, oil on canvas, 39 x 32, 1908
Bequest of Mrs. Katherine Dexter McCormick NPG. 68.13

ALEXANDER GRAHAM BELL *Hermes to the Silent World* 1847-1922

Soon after Alexander Graham Bell patented his telephone in 1876 he became involved in some six hundred law suits, all of which he won. Had Bell simply been the first to invent a practical telephone he would still have earned respect, but he was one of the most versatile men in American history. At one time or another he was physiologist and anatomist, professor of elocution, inventor, magazine publisher, and founder of vast economic enterprises. The real key to his career, however, is his work with the deaf.

Scottish by birth, Bell came to Boston from Canada in 1870 to adapt his father's system of "Visible Speech" (symbols representing the position of vocal organs in speaking) for use in the first American day school for the deaf. His marriage to a deaf girl in 1877 deepened his commitment to helping those cut off from the world of sound. The telephone was simply an outgrowth of this lifelong interest. After his invention had made him wealthy, Bell devoted his fortune to research on the deaf and methods of overcoming the handicap. His later interests also included the National Geographic Society, of which he was president; improvements on Edison's phonograph; and aviation.

MOSES DYKAAR, marble, 23 high, 1922
Lent by National Collection of Fine Arts, Smithsonian Institution

GULICK

JOSEPH PULITZER *Progressive Press Lord*   **1847-1911**

Tall, scraggly, and hook-nosed — his enemies called him "Pull-it-Sir" — Joseph Pulitzer emigrated from Hungary in 1864 to serve in Lincoln's Union army. There he met Carl Schurz, a fellow immigrant, who helped him get started in the newspaper business after the war. Pulitzer, who was strongly competitive and insatiably curious, emerged from the rough-and-tumble journalism of his time with a great publishing empire. As owner of the *St. Louis Post-Dispatch* and New York *World*, he dominated turn-of-the-century journalism. He believed that "honesty is to a newspaper what virtue is to a woman" and saw the press as a medium of public education. He relied for a time, however, upon blaring headlines, pictures of crime and sex, and trumped-up atrocity tales to sell his newspapers.

Pulitzer's idealism and love of American democracy ran deeper than his passion for personal gain.

He personally used the editorial page to educate the masses to the possibilities of the American way of life, knowing from experience the limitations of life in autocratic Europe. As the organ of "the aristocracy of labor," the *World* advocated many antimonopolistic and humanitarian reforms. To perpetuate his system of journalism and to encourage public service, Pulitzer established, in his will, a school for young newspapermen at Columbia University and the Pulitzer prizes.

He was elected to the Missouri State House of Representatives and later to the United States Senate from New York, where he might have been a career politician if journalism had not dominated his life. Although nearly blind and a semi-invalid, he remained until his death a powerful figure with a keen interest in the world around him.

Lent by Joseph Pulitzer, Jr.
JOHN SINGER SARGENT, oil on canvas, 38¾ x 28¾, 1905

AUGUSTUS SAINT-GAUDENS *Heroic Sculptor* **1848-1907**

Augustus Saint-Gaudens dominated American sculpture in the last half of the nineteenth century, freeing it from the arid conventions of late neoclassicism. Yet, he was more interested in expressing universal themes in stone than in heading an American artistic revolution.

Saint-Gaudens — born in Dublin to a French shoemaker who emigrated to America when the son was still an infant — might well have claimed more than one country as home. After studying at Cooper Union and the National Academy of Design in New York, he left at nineteen for a prolonged stay in Europe. In Paris he received the rigorous training of the Beaux-Arts, and while in Rome he studied the naturalism of the Italian Renaissance. But instead of sculpting idealized classical nudes he began his Italian work with a

"Hiawatha" and went on to realistic portrait monuments of such Civil War figures as Admiral Farragut and General Sherman. Returning to America around 1877, he completed a number of important public commissions in major cities of the country. He was also instrumental in founding the National Academy of Design and the American Academy in Rome.

The accuracy and simple strength of his work, together with his exuberant personality and unfettered mind, won Saint-Gaudens many friends, some famous and others unknown. They included the architect Stanford White and fellow artists John LaFarge and William M. Chase, who is the subject of the relief portrait shown in this painting of the sculptor at work in his studio.

KENYON COX, oil on canvas, 33½ x 46⅞, 1908 (replica of life portrait, 1887)
Lent by The Metropolitan Museum of Art, Gift of Friends of the Sculptor, 1908

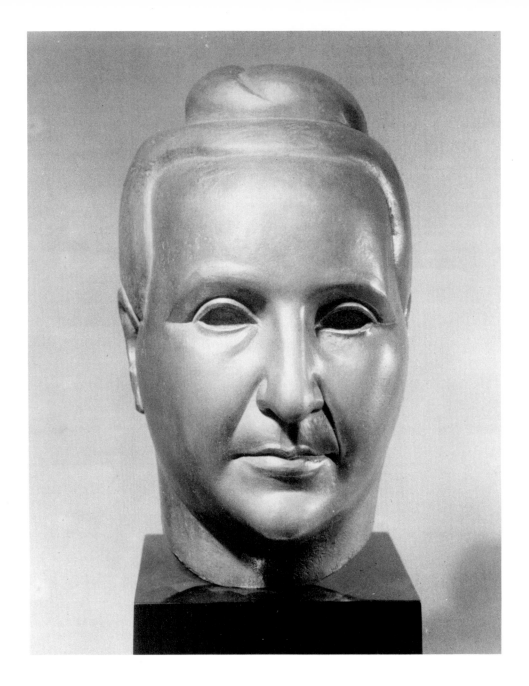

GERTRUDE STEIN *Oracle of the Lost Generation* 1874-1946

Gertrude Stein was a vigorous, headstrong woman with an appetite for life that drew people to her. Matisse, Picasso, Juan Gris, Ezra Pound, Sherwood Anderson, and Ernest Hemingway were among her close friends. With her brother Leo, she was an early and discriminating collector of modern French painting. While she chose exile from America in 1903, she welcomed to her Paris apartment two generations of American visitors, including soldiers of both World Wars. She was the tutelary genius of those American expatriates who, disillusioned after World War I, came to Europe in search of lost values; and she was the link between her fellow countrymen and the Euro-pean literary and artistic avant-garde.

Gertrude Stein's novels may not be remembered by many, but her experiments with the English language affected the prose style of several generations of writers. Influenced by her friend Picasso, and par-alleling the innovations of cubist painting, she peeled away the outmoded rhetoric of the nineteenth century to reach the simplest and most enduring locutions of the human mind. Through dislocation, fragmentation, and seemingly nonsensical repetition of words, her language became a distinctive voice of the twentieth century.

JACQUES LIPCHITZ, bronze, 13½ high, 1921
Lent by The Baltimore Museum of Art, Baltimore, Maryland, Cone Collection

The
American
Is . . .

. . . a Citizen and Sovereign

To have created a free government, over a continental area, without making a sacrifice of adequate efficiency or of liberty is the American achievement. It is a unique achievement in world history.

Sir Denis W. Brogan,
The American Character (1944)

Like so many of the institutions that have taken root and flourished in the United States, the one of self-government represents the conjunction of an ideal and practical opportunity. The concept of popular sovereignty finding its authority in a social compact — a concept that had originated in such protoypes as the Puritan church covenants and the theories of John Locke in the seventeenth century — was reaffirmed by the Declaration of Independence: ". . . Governments are instituted among men, deriving their just Powers from the consent of the governed . . . ." This instrument also established irrevocably the premise of the American political system that government is the servant of the citizen. In times of moral confusion or apathy, especially, the servant must assume active leadership, interpreting to the public its noblest will and destiny.

Deeply ingrained in the colonists' heritage was the even older British tradition that the ownership of land carried with it the right to participate in government. With seemingly unlimited land to be had for the taking, the larger part of the population of colonial America could vote and hold office. The average American male therefore has had a longer experience of successful self-government than any other citizen, not excluding even his British counterpart.

Citizenship and suffrage were legislated largely by the individual states to the Civil War, but as early as 1840 nearly every state had bestowed the vote on all white males. Then in 1868 and 1870 came the ennobling words of the Fourteenth and Fifteenth Amendments:

All persons born or naturalized in the United States ... are citizens of the United States.

The right of citizens of the United States to vote shall not be denied or abridged ... on account of race, color, or previous condition of servitude.

In 1920 women also became fully participating members of the body politic. Henceforth, by right of birth or through declaration of intent, all citizens had the means of exercising sovereignty.

Lawmakers

The American holds firmly to the belief that under his government the sovereign power to make, enforce, and interpret the law rests ultimately in the citizen-voter. On this is based a system of government by elected representatives, officials, and judges, and a body of law subject to referendum and repeal. In the ultimate tribunal of the vox populi, the people may raise one of its heroes to the highest power and privilege, but they reserve the final power and privilege of unseating him through carefully established safeguards and precedents.

Based as it is on the clear principle of government by the governed, the democratic process, in the mind of the average American, is a simple one within the competence of any intelligent citizen. The concept of rotation in office was written into the Articles of Confederation, which limited the number of terms a Congressman might serve; into those state constitutions that prohibit governors from succeeding themselves; and into the Twenty-Second Amendment, which limits a President to two elected terms. The original purpose of rotation in office was not merely to prevent entrenched political power but to give more citizens the opportunity of serving in public office. The same insistence upon popular participation in government and lawmaking lies behind the election of judges in many jurisdictions and the frequent demand that public juries treat of the law as well as the fact in court cases.

Always rather self-conscious about his role as a sovereign citizen, the American once more has joined idealism to practicality. The leaders of the Revolutionary generation and the early national period, in particular, felt that they were working out their destiny under the skeptical scrutiny of the rest of the world and that they held in their hands the precious future of republicanism. "We stand, the latest, and if we fail, probably the last experiment of self-government by the people," wrote Justice Joseph Story early in the nineteenth century. In political matters, as in most other areas, however, the American has been more practical than theoretical. The written constitution, the constitutional convention, the federal system, judicial review — all were ingenious solutions to practical problems encountered in everyday life.

The American has a great respect for law, but he also has a long tradition of lawlessness and violence. He often uses lawbreaking as a method of lawmaking or, as he explains it, "takes the law into his own hands." Especially on the frontier the American has defied the law and had recourse to violence, as did the posse under a self-appointed

vigilante. The Ku Klux Klan, the feuding family mem-
bers in the Appalachians, the assassin of a President, those
who practice civil disobedience — all, in their several
ways, are making their own law, and in that respect they
may be considered characteristically American. At the
same time the classic instance of the "prohibition amend-
ment" shows that no law is enforceable, no authority effec-
tive, without the support of majority public opinion. When
laws are so unpopular they cannot be enforced, they are
modified or repealed.

The American is typically apathetic in his role as citizen-
sovereign. Although self-government has led to universal
suffrage, public education, and, finally, the protection of
minority groups, it has as often produced indifference or
complacency, separatism or intolerance, demagogy or
diffidence. Politics — the least honored of the professions
— on the regional and urban level has too often been
jealously dominated by special interest groups eager to
promote their own welfare by the most expedient means.
Only during a presidential compaign do Americans awake
from their political listlessness to participate as spectators
and, through their exercise of the vote, as players in their
favorite national game.

SIR WILLIAM BERKELEY *Royal Governor of Virginia* **1606-1677**

Although he spent nearly half of his long life in Virginia, Sir William Berkeley was never an American; he represents, however, the continuity of English law in the new country. In 1642 he was appointed by the King of England Governor of Virginia, then England's only royal colony. A courtier and cavalier, he was at first the "darling of the people," for he showed great concern for the welfare of the colony. But he had been sent, like other royal governors, with secret instructions to make the colony profitable to the mother country. Conflict with colonists seeking their own fortunes was therefore inevitable. Berkeley found the locally elected colonial assemblies ingenious in thwarting the royal will through their control of taxation and appropriations. By providing the colonists with valuable training in political strategy, the royal governor unintentionally helped them prepare for self-government.

Deposed during the Cromwellian revolution and crushed by the execution of King Charles I, Berkeley returned to office with the Restoration in 1660, bitter and reactionary. His arbitrary rule coupled with a depression in the colony and trouble with the Indians brought on Bacon's Rebellion of 1676. Berkeley's vindictive handling of this uprising caused him to be recalled to England where he died broken in spirit.

SIR PETER LELY, oil on canvas, 50 x 40, not dated
Lent by Maurice du Pont Lee

CHARLES CALVERT   *Royal Anachronism*   **1637-1715**

Charles Calvert, third Lord Baltimore, represents a dynasty of colonial proprietors unparalleled in America. Granted the most extensive power ever conceded by the English Crown, the Calvert family ruled the Colony of Maryland for 137 years except for two short intervals. Yet the near-monarchal regime was doomed to failure, depending as it did on a feudal rent system in a region where free land was abundant. Furthermore, as the desire for self-government grew stronger each successive proprietor found it more difficult to hold his realm together.

Calvert governed the colony as an absolute lord from 1675 to 1689. More aware than his predecessors of the conditions, needs, and character of his people, Calvert nevertheless fell short of solving their problems or understanding the new spirit of representative government. He spent most of his time crushing opposition to his authority and resisting infringement on his territorial rights. A Catholic in a largely Protestant colony, he and his government were overthrown by a Protestant rebellion. When at the same time King William III withdrew his royal support, Calvert lost his princely authority and became a mere landlord of Maryland soil.

GODFREY KNELLER, oil on canvas, 89 x 57, not dated
Lent by The Enoch Pratt Free Library, Baltimore, Maryland

ROGER SHERMAN *Revolutionary Constitutionalist* 1721-1793

The only man to sign the Articles of Association of 1774, the Declaration of Independence, the Articles of Confederation, and the Constitution, Roger Sherman was a cautious revolutionary who weighed carefully his decision to support the cause of independence. Once decided, he applied himself diligently to his task. He labored long in the Continental Congresses at the tedious committee work that resulted in the Declaration of Independence and the Articles of Confederation. Seeing that the young nation was still beset with problems after independence, he attended the Federal Convention in 1787. There he worked hard on the new Constitution, to which he contributed the Great Compromise, providing representation by state in the Senate and by population in the House of Representatives.

A heavy, awkward man, Sherman was often ridiculed for his clumsiness. He never forgot his humble beginnings as a cobbler in a small Connecticut town or his lack of a formal education. But few men of aristocratic origins and formal learning could boast of his accomplishments. With a brilliant, incisive mind and a sharp wit, this self-taught lawyer and self-made businessman could argue with John Adams over the nature of government and discuss religion with the best New England theologians. Adams described him respectfully as "an old Puritan, as honest as an angel and as firm in the cause of American Independence as Mount Atlas." It was pious, practical men like Sherman who undertook the most daring political experiment of the century — self-government by a free people — and made it work.

RALPH EARL, oil on canvas, 64⅝ x 49⅝, about 1777
Lent by Yale University Art Gallery, New Haven, Connecticut

JOHN HANCOCK *Lawbreaker*   **1737-1793**

John Hancock, the most honored smuggler in history, was the wealthiest merchant in Boston in 1768. Refusing to pay the duty on wine imported from Spain in his ship *Liberty*, he locked the British customs official in the cabin while the illicit cargo was unloaded. When the British seized the sloop, Hancock became an instant celebrity and a popular leader of the rebellion against the Crown. He and Samuel Adams were wanted men in April 1775 when British troops, sent to arrest them and seek out hidden arms, encountered American patriots in the first battles of the Revolution, at Lexington and Concord.

As president of the Continental Congress, Hancock's name headed the list of signers to the Declaration of Independence, which stated that Britain, not the colonies, had violated fundamental law. Inevitably Hancock became a constitution-maker at the 1780 convention, which wrote the original state constitution for Massachusetts. He served as the first state governor under that frame of government.

John Hancock did everything with a flourish. Others smuggled, but he was colorful enough to incite a mob to defend his sloop. Others signed the Declaration of Independence, but his bold signature is the one which everyone remembers. Handsome, something of a dandy, he risked his fortune and life to be free of laws he had had no voice in making.

JOHN SINGLETON COPLEY, oil on canvas, 49½ x 40½, 1765
Lent by the City of Boston, deposited at the Museum of Fine Arts, Boston

FREDERICK AUGUSTUS CONRAD MUHLENBERG *Lawmaker's Lawmaker* 1750-1801

The first Speaker of the House of Representatives, Frederick Muhlenberg, began his career in the pulpit. His father, Henry Melchior Muhlenberg, organizer of the Lutheran Church in America, had gently led his son in his own theological footsteps; but church walls could not contain Frederick's pioneer initiative. The Revolution helped him decide on a political career. A representative from Pennsylvania to the Continental Congress, he presided over his home state's ratification convention in 1787. Muhlenberg went on to serve in the first four United States Congresses and was Speaker of the House in the first and third.

Muhlenberg was chosen Speaker because, as a moderate representing a strong central state, he could be trusted to exercise a stabilizing influence. In 1795 he cast the deciding vote in favor of Jay's Treaty with the British, believing it necessary for the sake of peace. His vote was so unpopular that it brought his national political career to an end. Although he retired from Congress to become a businessman and civil servant, he remained a dominant force in Pennsylvania politics until his death.

JOSEPH WRIGHT, oil on canvas, 47 x 37, 1790
Lent by Mrs. George Brooke III

JOHN MARSHALL *Lawmaker by Judicial Decision* **1755-1835**

The United States Supreme Court has often been charged with writing new legislation in the process of interpreting existing law. Roars of disapproval greeted decision after decision handed down by the Court in the nearly thirty-five years (1801-1835) that John Marshall was Chief Justice.

Marshall was determined to assert the supremacy of the national government over the states and to protect private property. He himself therefore wrote most of the decisions of his day involving constitutional issues. In proclaiming the right of the Supreme Court to declare acts of Congress unconstitutional, he raised the Supreme Court to a position of power equal to that of the two other branches of government. Without judicial review, the splendid new idea of a written constitution would in time have become meaningless.

This august architect of the young nation's constitutional law was a lanky, horseshoe-pitching frontiersman with little legal training. Convivial and easygoing, he and the other Justices often lived together in the same boardinghouse while the Court was in session. But when he read an important decision in the tiny courtroom under the Capitol, with Washington society crowding in attendance, he made an impressive appearance. Philadelphia's famed Liberty Bell cracked while tolling the passing of the great jurist in 1835.

JAMES R. LAMBDIN, oil on canvas, 36 x 28, 1832
Gift of Andrew Mellon   NPG.42.14

JAMES KENT *American Blackstone*   1763-1847

James Kent's decisions and commentaries on United States law strongly influenced American legal development. During the first quarter of the nineteenth century he formulated, systematized, and expounded common law and equity jurisprudence so extensively that his writings are still influential in the courts. A strong conservative, Kent reinterpreted the legal system inherited from England in the light of the United States Constitution and American experience. He believed strongly in the traditional rights of individuals under equity as distinguished from those provided by statute, and fought to secure these rights within the framework of the law. In constitutional law Kent's writings "foreshadowed Marshall," but Kent was also an outstanding authority on international and municipal jurisprudence.

Kent had decided on a law career when at the age of fifteen he read Blackstone's *Commentaries on the Law of England,* the classical English law treatise. Appointed the first professor of law at Columbia University in 1793, he subsequently expanded his lectures into his own *Commentaries on American Law.* More extensive than Blackstone's, this enduring achievement has made him the "father of American jurisprudence." Kent also served as judge and chief justice of the Supreme Court of New York and chancellor of that state's Chancery Court. In these positions he preserved the best features of English law while elevating American judicial conduct by his own example of dignity, probity, and intellectual eminence.

Daniel Huntington, oil on canvas, 30 x 25, not dated
NPG.67.47

DANIEL WEBSTER *Voice of Gold*   **1782-1852**

It seems to me to be plain that, in the absence of military force, political power naturally and necessarily goes into the hands which hold the property.

In these words Daniel Webster, unquestionably the greatest orator in a generation of orators, spoke as always in the interest of New England's business community. Using the full resources of his melodious voice and dramatic delivery, he pled for the sanctity of contract before the Supreme Court, advocated a protective tariff in the Senate, and, as Secretary of State, negotiated a treaty with England. No doubt he was sincere when he declaimed, "Liberty *and*

Union, now and forever, one and inseparable." But New England manufacturers also loved the Union. Hailing him the "godlike Daniel" because of his commanding presence, they more than once openly raised a large sum to pay off his debts so that this lover of luxury could continue to represent their interests in the Senate without sacrifice.

With his monumental egotism and insatiable ambition, Webster hoped to become President. In an earlier age he might have succeeded; but by the time he had become a public figure the extension of suffrage to all white males precluded the election of a man with an unconcealed taste for fine wine and elegant furnishings.

G. P. A. HEALY, oil on canvas, 50½ x 40, 1846
Gift of Andrew Mellon   NPG.42.10

CHARLES SUMNER   *Wrathful Reformer*   **1811-1874**

Charles Sumner crusaded in Congress for the most enlightened causes of his day. As Senator from Massachusetts from 1851 until his death he championed the abolition of slavery and the outlawry of war. He is remembered principally for his struggle to obtain rights for Negroes, but he also fought for civil service and prison reforms.

Despite his dedication and efforts, his career was marred by rancor and malice. A powerful orator, his furious invective against the South caused Preston S. Brooks of South Carolina to attack him violently with a cane on the Senate floor. After the Civil War he was the chief proponent of "radical" reconstruction, a policy of revenge designed more to hurt the South than

to benefit the United States. He despised President Andrew Johnson so thoroughly that he took a leading role in the impeachment trial. Sumner's career demonstrates dramatically that in a democratic system the personality of a single citizen may affect the course of history.

The contradictions in Sumner's public record are tied to the violent conflicts in his own nature. A tireless champion of human justice and equality, he took a perverse delight in the role of martyr. Having created a host of antagonists by his savage vindictiveness, he lapsed into fits of self-loathing and depression. Charles Sumner was a New England Puritan gone sour.

WILLIAM MORRIS HUNT, oil on canvas, 27 x 22, between 1874 and 1879
Lent by The Metropolitan Museum of Art, A. B. Lazarus Fund

HENRY CABOT LODGE *Imperialist in the Senate* **1850-1924**

Henry Cabot Lodge, a Boston Brahmin, had the self-confidence that came from a distinguished ancestry, a Harvard education, and a circle of wealthy, influential friends. A master politician, he began his thirty-seven years in Congress in 1887 as a political outsider and rose to senior member of the Senate and head of the Republican Party. He felt amply qualified to determine what was best for America, and accordingly took full advantage of the constitutional provision for the United States Senate to participate in foreign policy making.

Lodge as a young man had advanced views on foreign affairs for the nineteenth century and with his friend Theodore Roosevelt sought for the United States a large role in world affairs. An Anglophile, he in-

fluenced his own country to emulate British naval and imperial power in order to have a voice in international councils.

Ironically, Lodge is best remembered for defeating the League of Nations Covenant in the Senate after World War I. He saw the merits of President Wilson's dream of world organization, but out of fear for American sovereignty and the wish to safeguard it he proposed reservations to the Covenant. Since he met in Wilson an arrogance equal to his own, compromise between the two was impossible and the League failed of adoption. The man who prepared America for world leadership in the nineteenth century came to be regarded in the twentieth as a cautious isolationist.

JOHN SINGER SARGENT, oil on canvas, 50 x 34, 1890
Gift of Henry Cabot Lodge, Jr.   NPG. 67.58

CHARLES EVANS HUGHES *Judicial Moderator* **1862-1948**

Charles Evans Hughes presided over the United States Supreme Court that in 1935 and 1936 tore great holes in the early "New Deal" fashioned by President Franklin D. Roosevelt to expedite recovery from the Great Depression. By a series of sweeping decisions, the Court declared unconstitutional federal and state legislation by which the government was to participate directly in the national economy. Angry New Dealers, seeing in Hughes an arch reactionary, struck back in 1937 with an unsuccessful attempt to "pack" the Court by increasing the number of justices and forcing early retirements.

Yet, the facts of Hughes' long career show that he had been a progressive Governor of New York, a liberal Associate Justice of the Supreme Court, and an internationalist Secretary of State under President Harding. Committed to preserving the traditional flexibility of the law through judicial interpretation, he once said, "We are under a Constitution, but the Constitution is what the judges say it is . . ."

In the 1930s Hughes saw the Court's role as a curb on emergency legislation hastily devised to meet rapid and sweeping social change. He held the court to its established role of restraining the executive and legislative branches of government in their reaction to immediate crises and political pressures. At the same time, as presiding judge, he had the task of holding together a sharply divided court appointed in another era.

PHILIP DE LASZLO, oil on canvas, 44 x 36, 1921
Lent by Chauncey L. Waddell

71

Liberators and Crusaders

A compulsive reformer, the American can always see a way in which conditions—and people—can be improved. He cannot rest until the wilderness is tamed and the wasteland reclaimed, the benighted enlightened, and the lost soul saved—sometimes without regard to the consequences of his good intentions.

The Puritans who settled Massachusetts in 1629 left comfortable homes in a known world not only to seek freedom but to found the ideal state as an example to erring peoples left behind. The faith which inspired them rested upon three convictions: that the redeeming work was absolutely necessary, that they knew precisely how it should be done, and that they were eminently capable of doing it — with the help of God. Americans of all creeds ever since have felt a sacred mission to create a perfect society and to bestow or impose it upon others.

As a reformer and missionary, the American has been at his best and at his worst. He is admirable in his devotion to great causes, but he can be condescending to those he considers less fortunate or less emancipated than himself. In him self-deprecation may be another manifestation of Puritan self-righteousness. He sometimes forgets his unparalleled opportunity to build a nation with the abundant resources of a nearly empty continent, the technology of the Industrial Revolution, and a population "disposed to democracy by the self-reliant temper of uprooted pioneers."

Those Americans who engaged in noble works have varied as dramatically as the causes they have served. Cardinal Gibbons, a clergyman, appeared as labor's champion; General Pershing, the professional soldier, as the emissary of liberty. In a country with a high level of literacy, the written word has served equally the revolutionary pamphleteer, the muckraking journalist, and the professional agitator. And the amateur crusader of an earlier day more recently has yielded his role to the professionally trained. Likewise, the weapons and strategy have varied with the reformer: from the sword of Lafayette to the pen of Horace Greeley; and from Lucretia Mott, who moved forward on several fronts at once, to Dorothea Dix, who fought with single purpose and alone.

Among the multitude of immigrants, hungry for land and opportunity, who came to America were a sprinkling of idealists and romantics. Many remained to help make the dream a reality; others, like Kościuszko and Lafayette, returned with new hope for their own lands.

SAMUEL ADAMS *Professional Agitator*   **1722-1803**

Samuel Adams was a vigorous radical and skillful revolutionary. From 1765 on he worked single-mindedly at rousing the American colonists to assert their independence. To inflame their minds he magnified a minor incident into the "Boston Massacre" and dramatized resistance to British taxation with the "Boston Tea Party." To organize resistance more effectively, he urged the merchants to sign nonimportation agreements against British goods and promoted Committees of Correspondence in all the colonies to form an information network. Although he had not foreseen a complete break with Great Britain, he did as much as any statesman to make it inevitable.

Copley's portrait shows Adams as he sternly challenged Governor Hutchinson of Massachusetts the day after the Boston Massacre, which took place 5 March 1770. In his right hand Adams is holding a paper inscribed "Instructions of Town Boston," while he points with his left to the "Charter of William & Ma[ry] to Massachusetts." Recalling the confrontation a year later, he wrote: "It was then, if fancy deceived me not, I saw his knees to tremble. I thought I saw his face grow pale (and I enjoyed the sight) at the appearance of the determined citizens peremptorily demanding the redress of grievances."

With quavering voice, shaking hand, and shabby clothes, Adams in actuality was not a heroic figure. Unable to make the barest living, he was in debt and dependent on charity much of his life. After the Revolution he quickly lost touch with the mainstream of political life and was unpopular as Governor of Massachusetts. It seemed that he was successful only at revolutionary agitations, but at this he was supremely good.

JOHN SINGLETON COPLEY, oil on canvas, 50 x 40¼, about 1770-1772
Lent by the City of Boston, deposited at the Museum of Fine Arts, Boston

THOMAS PAINE *Inveterate Revolutionary*   **1737-1809**

The constant critic is never beloved for long, even in America where self-criticism is a national habit.

Thomas Paine arrived in America in 1774 already branded a dangerous man because he had petitioned Parliament for better wages for his fellow excisemen. In January 1776 there appeared in Philadelphia an anonymous pamphlet titled "Common Sense" that called upon Americans to free themselves from British rule, to end the absurdity of a continent tied to an island, and to establish the ideal republic as an example to the rest of the world. The author, who thus proposed independence when few had dared to think it, was Thomas Paine. He went on to serve the American cause both as a common soldier and an indefatigable propagandist. The fourteen issues of the *American Crisis* which he published during the war did much to bolster the patriots' morale in "times that try men's souls."

Soon after the War of Independence Paine was in France participating in the French Revolution and in England trying to create an English revolution. Meanwhile, *The Age of Reason* (1794-1796), a deistic work rejecting Christianity, and a public letter denouncing the conservatism of the Washington administration had destroyed his honored position in America.

Citizen of Great Britain by birth, of the United States by immigration, and of France by vote of the National Assembly in 1792, Paine died in New York, a pariah in all three countries. It was well that he had declared, "My country is the world, and my religion is to do good."

JOHN WESLEY JARVIS, oil on canvas, 25¾ x 20½, about 1805
Lent by the National Gallery of Art, Washington, D. C., Gift of Miss Marian B. Maurice

TADEUSZ ANDRZEJ BONAWENTURA KOŚCIUSZKO *Hero of Two Worlds* 1746-1817

Tadeusz Kościuszko left his native Poland to defend liberty in the American Revolution, where his skill as an engineer was useful in constructing fortifications from Ticonderoga to Charleston. Unlike Lafayette, Kościuszko sought no glory. Thomas Jefferson remembered him as a man with a single purpose, "the freedom and happiness of man." A true democrat in the service of an ideal, his enthusiasm inspired patriotic fervor in others.

Having seen the American people win their inde-

pendence, Kościuszko returned to Poland to arm the peasants and to lead them in a heroic but futile crusade for their own independence. Weak from two years in a Russian prison and still wearing bandages from a wound that never healed, he sat for this painting by Benjamin West while in London in 1797. That same year he returned to this country where he was received with quiet respect by all who had fought with him, but without the popular adulation accorded Lafayette.

BENJAMIN WEST, oil on panel, 12¼ x 17⅜, 1797
Lent by Allen Memorial Art Museum, Oberlin College, Oberlin, Ohio

MARQUIS DE LAFAYETTE   *Soldier for Human Rights*   1757-1834

Born into a venerable French family, Marie Joseph Paul Yves Roch Gilbert du Motier, Marquis de Lafayette, came to America at nineteen to find *la gloire* by fighting France's traditional enemy in the American Revolution. Although Congress and General Washington regarded him at first as another foreign mercenary, Lafayette's charm, enthusiasm, and willingness to serve without pay won their trust and a commission as major general in the American Army. Impetuous, he nevertheless fought with distinction, particularly during the Virginia campaign that led to Yorktown. The portrait shown here by Charles Willson Peale, commissioned by Washington and delivered to him in 1781, shows Lafayette wearing his Continental Army uniform. On the table is a paper with writing which is believed to read, in part, "Geo. Washington Mt. Vernon Va."

America left its mark on Lafayette. What began as

a youthful adventure changed the course of his life. The young aristocrat returned to France to become an ardent champion of the rights of man and a leader in the revolutions of 1787 and 1830. Unfortunately Lafayette never fulfilled the role he saw for himself as the Washington of France.

Although Jefferson noted his "canine thirst for popularity and fame," the American public never perceived Lafayette's failings. To them he remained always the dashing young marquis who came from a foreign land to lay his fortune and services at their feet. On his first return to America in 1784 Lafayette was given a jubilant welcome and honorary citizenship by several of the states. When he returned again in the 1820s, a period of exuberant nationalism for the young nation, he had become a symbol of the Revolution and of the quest for freedom that linked two great nations.

CHARLES WILLSON PEALE, oil on canvas, 40 x 49, 1779
Lent by Washington and Lee University, Lexington, Virginia

LILLIAN BRISTOL

LUCRETIA COFFIN MOTT *Mother of Movements* **1793-1880**

"Practical godliness," according to William Lloyd Garrison, was the force behind Lucretia Mott's adoption of movements to free Negoes from slavery, drunkards from drink, and the world from constant warfare.

Used to speaking — and being listened to — in Quaker meetings, Lucretia Mott's celebrated temper flared when she was not allowed on platforms elsewhere; she was furious when refused admission to the World's Anti-Slavery Convention in London in 1840. Finding her influence limited because of her sex and concluding that women as well as slaves needed emancipation, she helped promote the first women's rights convention, held at Seneca Falls, New York, in 1848. Her husband presided.

Usually wearing an unadorned slate-gray silk dress, she walked with back straight, and with her cameo-like features perfectly composed, through the taunting mobs that rioted against her radical ideas. But with six children and a full homelife, she was not wedded to her causes like Dorothea Dix. Nor did she limit her activities to what she herself could accomplish. Many of the movements she organized had little success until long after her death.

JOSEPH KYLE, oil on canvas, 30 x 25, not dated
Lent by Mrs. Alan Valentine

DOROTHEA LYNDE DIX *The Incensed Individual* **1802-1887**

Personal indignation at cruelty to the insane and feebleminded compelled Dorothea Lynde Dix to conduct a one-woman crusade, with the exclamation point as her weapon. "I myself have seen . . ." she wrote of the brutal treatment in jails and almshouses. Unlike Lucretia Mott, she was not a feminist. Gentle and dignified in manner, she never spoke to male legislative bodies, but quietly persuaded influential members to present her petitions. More than a dozen new or improved mental hospitals were established at her behest, including St. Elizabeths in Washington. Not content with describing barbaric conditions and agitating for reform, she went abroad to study methods of treatment being used successfully in Paris.

Her response to need was always immediate action. Two days after the outbreak of the Civil War she was in Washington offering her services as a nurse, and throughout the war she worked as "Superintendent of Women Nurses." Louisa May Alcott, one of the volunteer nurses who served under her, found Miss Dix "rather strange" but kindly. The surgeon general thought her a sentimental nuisance because she insisted on clean bandages and solicited preserved fruit to prevent scurvy among the wounded. From the end of the war until her death at eighty-five she worked constantly on behalf of her hospitals.

SAMUEL BELL WAUGH, oil on canvas, 30 x 25, 1868
Lent by Saint Elizabeths Hospital, Washington, D. C.

HORACE GREELEY *Crusading Editor* 1811-1872

In an era of personal journalism when newspapers were unrivaled in molding public opinion, Horace Greeley was a master of the editorial craft. Founder and for thirty years editor of the *New York Tribune*, Greeley made it one of the great liberal newspapers in the middle years of the nineteenth century.

Few reforms escaped his advocacy. His trenchant editorials condemned slavery, capital punishment, unrestricted sale of liquor, and monopoly; he championed women's rights, cooperative shops, labor unions, and, during Reconstruction, full citizenship for the Negro. Often easily taken in, his compassion and breadth of concern nevertheless made him the archetype of the earnest moral reformer of his period.

Beloved and admired by his fellow radicals, Greeley was usually regarded with tolerant amusement by those who disagreed with him. But when he ran for President in 1872 as the candidate of the splinter Liberal Republican Party, affectionate ridicule became vicious derision. Greeley remarked that he wondered whether he was running for the Presidency or the penitentiary. Badly defeated in the popular vote and grieving for his wife who had died during the campaign, he returned to the *Tribune* only to find his control usurped. He died insane before the electoral vote was counted.

Thomas Nast, who painted this caricature for London's *Vanity Fair* at the height of the campaign, did much with his venomous cartoons in American publications to convince American voters that Greeley was a blundering buffoon unfit for the nation's highest office.

THOMAS NAST, watercolor on toned paper, 12 x 7, 1872
Gift of the Trustees of the National Portrait Gallery, London, England NPG.64.2

FREDERICK DOUGLASS *Humanitarian* **1817?-1895**

People had difficulty believing that Frederick Douglass, with his commanding presence and rich voice, was an escaped slave. To answer the question "Why am I a slave?" he wrote *Narrative of the Life of Frederick Douglass* (1845). "It was not *color,* but *crime,* not *God,* but *man*" — he observed — that explained the institution of slavery; but what man had done might be undone. Intelligent and independent, Douglass had fled his master in Maryland in 1838 and settled in Massachusetts, where he became an important figure in the New England Anti-Slavery Society. He finally purchased his own freedom several years after his book had been published.

At first Douglass saw emancipation only as physical freedom. After a trip to Europe, where he received an enthusiastic welcome from liberal sympathizers, his understanding of Negro liberation broadened to include social equality, economic opportunity, and, above all, self-respect. Composed and dignified in the midst of white extremists, whether for or against slavery, he issued a newspaper, the *North Star,* on behalf of his race; helped Harriet Beecher Stowe establish an industrial school for Negro children; and counseled with John Brown. He urged Negroes to support the North during the Civil War, and he was called into conference by Lincoln. A tireless supporter of woman suffrage and other social reforms, his efforts were not confined to Negro causes. His final years were spent with increasing honor. He was successively secretary of the Santo Domingo Commission, marshall and recorder of deeds of the District of Columbia, and, finally, United States minister to Haiti.

J. W. HURN, cabinet photograph, oval, 7⅜ x 5⅜, not dated
Lent by the Library of Congress

JAMES CARDINAL GIBBONS *The Concerned Prelate* **1834-1921**

The labor movement in the United States followed a different course from that in countries which had become industrialized earlier. James Cardinal Gibbons, the second American to become a Roman Catholic Cardinal, generally is credited with taking the step which brought the change about.

In 1887 Gibbons, a native of Baltimore and son of Irish immigrants, journeyed to Rome to receive his Cardinal's red hat. While there he persuaded Pope Leo XIII not to condemn Catholic participation in the Knights of Labor, a semisecret organization which had achieved considerable success as a national work-ingman's organization. As a result, the Catholic immigrants who flocked to the growing industrial cities and into American factories were free to join labor unions with the blessing of the Catholic Church. The strong stand of the Church against socialism was at least partly responsible for the conservatism of American labor, which accepted free enterprise and long remained largely nonpolitical.

Gibbons also felt that in America the Catholic Church must uphold the separation of church and state and that Catholic ethnic groups must forget their national origins and become *American* Catholics.

FLORENCE MACKUBIN, watercolor on ivory, 4 x 3, 1902
Lent by the Walters Art Gallery, Baltimore, Maryland

JOHN J. PERSHING *Professional Soldier*

1860-1948

"Lafayette, we are here." The American Expeditionary Force had arrived in France in 1917 with a mission to make the world safe for democracy. Its commander, General John J. Pershing, was once more the dutiful agent in one of the American people's real or rationalized campaigns of liberation. His early career belonged to the final years of "Manifest Destiny," the nineteenth-century crusade to spread the benefits of American democracy across the continent. To civilize and extend the settled areas of the country, "Black Jack" Pershing had served in expeditions to force the Plains Indians of the Southwest onto reservations. He next fought in the American effort to free Cuba from Spanish rule during the Spanish-American War in

1898. The Philippines, wrested from Spain at the same time, expected immediate independence, but Pershing was sent to establish American "guidance" over the unwilling islanders.

A matter-of-fact traditionalist, Pershing found himself an agent in American crusades because, as a career Army officer, he was in the right place at the right time. In 1917 he seemed to be the only man with the experience and professional skill to create an army from an unequipped, ill-trained mass of recruits and to lead it to victory. He may have seen himself only as an excellent soldier, but to Americans at home he was the valiant leader of an army of liberation.

SIR WILLIAM ORPEN, oil on canvas, 36 x 30, about 1918
Gift of the International Business Machines Corporation NPG.68.12

HARRY L. HOPKINS *Trained Social Worker*   **1890-1946**

Relief, recovery, and reform were the planks that Harry L. Hopkins masterminded for Franklin Roosevelt's platform in the campaign of 1932. Representing a new breed of reformers who held college degrees in social work, Hopkins served his apprenticeship in the settlement houses of New York City. As chairman of New York's Temporary Emergency Relief Administration while Roosevelt was governor, he formulated programs for direct relief of the unemployed by the State. When Roosevelt became President he called on Hopkins to set up similar programs on a national scale, as the federal government for the first time assumed an active responsibility for the social welfare of the American people. His relief projects through the

Works Progress Administration and other federal agencies helped pull the United States out of the depths of the Great Depression.

Lean, restless, and like an "ill-used Raggedy Andy," Hopkins was driven by a perpetual need for action. Even while dying of cancer he worked loyally and doggedly for his beloved President Roosevelt. His influence as Roosevelt's confidant penetrated into every branch of the executive office. During World War II he was catapulted into the demanding job of military liaison between the President and the Allied leaders. Winston Churchill aptly described Hopkins as a "crumbling lighthouse from which there shone the beams that led great fleets to harbor."

REUBEN NAKIAN, bronze, 26⅜ high, including base, not dated
Lent by The Museum of Modern Art, New York, New York, Gift of Charles Abrams

Defenders
and
Peacemakers

Inevitably the sovereign citizen has had to be a citizen-soldier, for a free state bestows on him both the right and the obligation to bear arms in defense of his country. But when the dictates of private conscience, which he holds even more dear, conflict with his public duty he may refuse this obligation or, like Robert E. Lee, enlist in an alien cause. Occasionally warlike but seldom military, the American has preferred to rely through most of his history on local voluntary militia or a temporary army of citizen-conscripts. Only since World War II has he accepted as necessary a large professional military establishment.

The American, often last in war, is by conviction first in peace, which he cherishes as the birthright of a new land. He is a reluctant dragon that can be persuaded to fight only under the emblem of a cause in which he can be made to believe. Confident that he lives in the world's most favored region and enjoys the finest political system, he is ready to defend these advantages against all who appear to threaten them, even against his own government if he believes it has forsaken the purposes assigned it in the Declaration of Independence and the Constitution. In our time he has assumed responsibility for defending democratic governments of other nations and has prescribed institutions similar to his own to cure the ills of strange and distant lands.

JEFFERY AMHERST   *Soldier of the King*   **1717-1797**

Lord Jeffery Amherst was the last commander in chief of British forces in America during the French and Indian War. After nearly two centuries of struggle for control of eastern North America, France and England in 1754 entered into the hostilities that were to decide the conflict. Until 1758 the war had proved disastrous for England; but in that year William Pitt the Elder, who had been appointed Prime Minister to end these reverses, ordered Amherst, James Wolfe, and two other able young officers to America. Amherst took Louisbourg on Cape Breton Island, the first English victory in the war, and went on to plan the campaigns which won Quebec and Montreal. By 1760 when Canada had become a part of the British Empire, there

was no longer any question as to which country would control North America.

Amherst was a competent, cautious professional soldier, but his contemporaries found him pompous and cold. Although several New England towns were named in his honor, he had no love for America. He was named governor of Virginia but he never lived there; as soon as possible he returned to England and his country house in Kent. At the outbreak of the War of Independence, he refused to fight again on the American continent. Appointed commander in chief of British forces in England in 1778 and again in 1793, he became a favorite of George III but an unpopular figure with the English people.

JOSEPH BLACKBURN, oil on canvas, 32 x 26¼, 1758
Lent by Mrs. Frederic R. Pratt

NATHANAEL GREENE *A General for All Occasions*   **1742-1786**

Nathanael Greene, a Quaker iron forger from Rhode Island, was one among scores of obscure Americans raised to positions of authority and fame by the fateful shots at Lexington and Concord. Aroused to patriotic action, he turned his back on his religious teachings to study military science. Greene soon became so well informed on military matters that he was raised to the command of Rhode Island's armed forces. Although he was a fledgling general, his organizational ability caught the attention of General Washington, who made him his right-hand man in building up a disciplined, well-equipped army. An excellent military strategist, he masterminded many of Washington's campaigns. As its spokesman he presented the Continental Army's needs to the Congress, and as quarter-master general helped supply those needs.

Greene was appointed to succeed General Gates — who had been disastrously defeated — as commander of the Southern Department and made there his greatest contribution. His men idolized him for he suffered many of their hardships. He ate the same coarse food, slept in damp tents, and sacrificed his personal fortune to buy their equipment. He was often in pain from an inflamed cast in his right eye, and he limped because of a stiff knee. Although the British continued to amass victories, Greene remained undaunted: "We fight, get beat, rise, and fight again." His long series of skillful maneuvers in South Carolina and Georgia led eventually to the final collapse of British power in America.

CHARLES WILLSON PEALE, oil on canvas, 22 x 19, 1783
Lent by Montclair Art Museum, Montclair, New Jersey

JOHN PAUL JONES *Sea Rogue*   1747-1792

John Paul Jones's skillful seamanship, daring, and zest for a good close-hand fight made him the most success-ful and famous naval hero of the American Revolution. In British coastal towns and across more than a few British quarterdecks the mention of his name was enough to strike terror. The Continental Congress honored him uniquely with a gold medal, as did the ladies of Paris salons with their reciprocated attentions.

Jones liked to call himself a "citizen of the world." He was born near Kirkbean, Scotland, as plain John Paul, a gardener's son. At thirteen, however, he went to sea where he learned his craft in merchant ships and slavers. In 1773, while captain of a merchantman, he was indicted for the murder of a seaman and took refuge in America, adding the alias "Jones" as a disguise. Appointed a lieutenant in the Continental Navy, he quickly advanced in rank and fame, princi-pally through his raids on the coasts of Britain and Ireland. On 23 September 1779, in the *Bonhomme Richard*, christened after Benjamin Franklin's pen name, he met the newer, more heavily armed British frigate *Serapis*. Under a harvest moon before an awed audience watching from the English coast, the two ships grappled to near mutual destruction before the *Serapis* struck her colors. For America the victory brought a new confidence. For the diminutive sea captain it brought the glory he had so long sought.

CHARLES WILLSON PEALE, oil on canvas, 21½ x 19, about 1781
Lent by Independence National Historical Park Collection, Philadelphia, Pennsylvania

HENRY CLAY *The Intemperate Moderator* 1777-1852

A self-educated Senator from Kentucky and perennial candidate for President, Henry Clay, "Gallant Harry of the West," made his famous statement "I'd rather be right than President" only after his last hope of the high office was gone. Even then, he commented dryly that the saying was "applauded beyond its merits."

Clay was an effective Speaker of the House, and later one of a great triumvirate of Senators that included John C. Calhoun and Daniel Webster. His countrymen gratefully nicknamed him the "Great Peacemaker" for his leadership in working out com-

promises on the slavery question. An advocate of gradual emancipation and a staunch Unionist, Clay sought to stave off civil war by reconciling extremists of the North and South.

Tall and loose-jointed, Clay had an expressive face, a wide mouth, and a chin which he described as "not remarkable." He was a lovable wit, a serious gambler, a connoisseur of fine horses and good liquor, and a charmer of ladies. His quick temper and fearlessness led this impetuous frontiersman into some well-publicized duels.

G. P. A. HEALY, oil on canvas, 30 x 25, 1845
Gift of Andrew Mellon NPG.47.7

STEPHEN DECATUR *Knight Avenger*   **1779-1820**

At the turn of the eighteenth century America embarked on a hazardous maritime trade of global extent. The ships that sailed under the Stars and Stripes carried no naval protection, making them easy prey to the Barbary corsairs off the North African coast. Since the European nations were engaged in the Napoleonic wars and offered little resistance to the pirates, the obvious remedy was to reconstitute the American Navy, nonexistent since the Revolution. Stephen Decatur joined the newly revived navy and set out with calm fortitude to avenge the depredations on American merchantmen. His skill in naval tactics and personal heroism enabled him to outmaneuver the pirate ships and destroy them piecemeal. Henceforth European and American merchant ships were no longer obliged to pay tribute for permission to sail the Mediterranean or to ransom their crews from Algerian dungeons. In the War of 1812 Decatur again fought for "freedom of the seas" in single-ship action against the British.

From his father, the elder Stephen Decatur, a Revolutionary privateer and captain in the naval war with France (1798-1800), Stephen had inherited his taste for perilous action at sea. A proud, daring youth, Decatur sought glory both for himself and his navy. Responding to a toast after the victory against the British, he voiced his ardent patriotism: "Our country . . . may she always be in the right; but our country, right or wrong." At forty-one he was killed in a duel when his sense of honor made him refuse to aim at a vengeful man who had poor eyesight.

GILBERT STUART, oil on canvas, 30¼ x 25¼, about 1815
Lent by Jonathan Bryan

JOHN C. CALHOUN   *Vindicator of States Rights*   **1782-1850**

Enthusiastic "War Hawk" in Congress during the War of 1812 and Vice President under John Quincy Adams and Andrew Jackson, John Calhoun was a national leader with reasonable hopes for the Presidency until loyalty to his native South Carolina made him a contentious sectionalist. In the bitter years after 1832, Calhoun sat in the United States Senate defending slavery and the Southern plantation system, already an anachronism.

In his later years he ridiculed the idea that all men were created equal and repudiated the Declaration of Independence. Possibly the most gifted political thinker the United States has produced, he constructed an impressive body of States Rights constitutional theory in a futile attempt to make the Union safe for slaveholders. His most celebrated stratagem was the doctrine of "nullification," permitting a convention of any state to declare a federal law "null, void, and no law" within that state.

This "cast iron man," tall, gaunt, and with piercing eye, silenced opponents with unanswerable logic and disciplined oratory. He remained lonely and austere in his intellectual eminence, inspiring much hatred and some reverence but little affection.

G. P. A. HEALY, oil on canvas, 30 x 25, about 1845
Lent by The Virginia Museum of Fine Arts, Richmond, Virginia

OLIVER HAZARD PERRY *Guardian of the Great Lakes* **1785-1819**

Oliver Perry, hero of the Battle of Lake Erie, won the first significant American naval victory in the War of 1812. He defeated the British on 10 September 1813 after performing the prodigious task of building a fleet of ships in the isolated port of Erie, Pennsylvania, and manning them with ill-trained frontiersmen. A master of laconic speech, he is famous for his dispatch to General William Henry Harrison following that battle: "We have met the enemy and they are ours." The Battle of Lake Erie was one of the few decisive victories in the war and marked the unprecedented capture of a British fleet by the American Navy.

Perry belonged to the second generation of a Rhode Island naval family. His father had served in the Revolution; and his younger brother, Matthew C. Perry, opened Japan to American trade. An educated man and a fine sailor, he was well versed in the exacting skills of a naval officer. His energy and his generous, impetuous temperament made him a popular officer, but they also got him into some notable arguments and one duel. He died of yellow fever at the age of thirty-four while on a diplomatic mission to Venezuela.

JOHN WESLEY JARVIS, oil on canvas, 31¼ x 26, not dated
Lent by The Detroit Institute of Arts, Gift of Dexter M. Ferry, Jr.

WINFIELD SCOTT   *Instrument of Manifest Destiny*   **1786-1866**

Winfield Scott, general-in-chief of the United States Army from 1841 to 1861, served the interests of America during fifty crucial years of Western expansion. For every President from Jefferson to Lincoln he undertook critical missions aimed at either preventing or winning wars. He pacified the "Nullifiers" in South Carolina, transported the Cherokees peaceably across the Mississippi, and settled border disputes with Canada. An excellent soldier, he played a major role in one of the few successful land operations against the British in the War of 1812. His victorious campaigns in the Mexican War confirmed the annexation of Texas and brought the cession of much of the Southwest.

Although Virginia-born, he remained loyal to the Union in the Civil War, and before retiring in 1861 he organized the defenses around Washington.

Despite his long years of devoted public service, Scott was often bitterly opposed by politicians and was never honored with election to the Presidency. The Whig Party nominated him for President in 1852, but he was overwhelmingly defeated by Franklin Pierce. Nicknamed "Old Fuss and Feathers" for his strict dress and pompous conduct, the six-foot, five-inch giant was too much in the military tradition of rugged independence and blunt speech to make a successful politician.

HENRY KIRKE BROWN, bronze, 28¾ high, not dated
Gift of Henry Kirke Bush-Brown   NPG.26.6

ROBERT E. LEE   *Defender of the Old Dominion*   **1807-1870**

With the coming of civil war between North and South, Robert E. Lee chose to defend Virginia rather than the Union. It was not an easy decision. He believed that slavery was a "moral and political evil" and that secession was "nothing but revolution," yet he could not free himself from emotional ties that bound him to his native Virginia. Refusing command of the United States Army, he placed his considerable military talents and West Point training at the disposal of the Confederate States of America, which eventually made him general-in-chief. Against impossible odds he kept an army in the field for four years but, when further resistance became futile, he surrendered gallantly.

The nobility of Lee's character and the gentleness of his nature, while not always assets in the pursuit of war, have contributed to the aura of chivalry which, in Southern minds, still surrounds the "lost cause."

Frank Buchser, the Swiss artist who painted this portrait from life, came to America after the Civil War to celebrate the victory of freedom and unity over bondage and secession. Although he did not endear himself to Southerners by this position, he held Robert E. Lee in high regard, later declaring that in his five years in this country the only great man he had met was Lee. In this sympathetic and convincing likeness, painted a year before Lee's death, the uniform and sword are laid aside, symbolizing the man of peace.

FRANK BUCHSER, oil on canvas, 54 x 40¼, 1869
Lent by Kunstmuseum, Berne, Switzerland, Property of the Swiss Confederation

WILLIAM TECUMSEH SHERMAN   *Scourge and Minister*   **1820-1891**

"War is war and not popularity-seeking." William Tecumseh Sherman's words to his Confederate opponent at Atlanta suggest the attitude that made him a successful Civil War commander and an object of Southern hatred. Behind his fanatic loyalty to the Union and Constitution were a stern sense of duty and professional thoroughness. A nervous but logical man, he stripped warfare of glory and chivalry, reducing it to the ruthless application of unqualified force to the objectives of grand strategy. In the calculated destruction of his march through the rich farmlands of Georgia and his subsequent campaign in the Carolinas, he demolished the economic base of the dying Confederacy and shattered the morale of its citizens. One of the first modern generals, Sherman anticipated twentieth-century total war in which soldier and citizen are equally vulnerable.

Sherman was born and raised in the quiet farm country of southeastern Ohio. He graduated from West Point in 1840, served without notable distinction as an officer until 1853, and was superintendent of a Louisiana military college (now Louisiana State Univer-

sity) when the Civil War began. In spite of his unexceptional background he quickly won Grant's confidence in the campaigns of 1862 and 1863 which culminated decisively in the capture of Vicksburg and control of the Mississippi River. Succeeding General Grant as commander in the West in 1864, he began at Chattanooga the methodical drive which carried him over the mountains to Atlanta, the ocean, and fame. Following the Civil War Sherman served as commanding general in the West, and from 1869 until his retirement in 1883 he was general-in-chief of the Army. With a long antipathy to politicians he found no difficulty in declining a proposed presidential draft in 1884.

In Frank Buchser's portrait, painted four years after the end of the Civil War, Sherman's dual nature and career are suggested not only by the contrast of his fixed, direct gaze and stern military pose with his pale face and lofty forehead but also by the symbolic sword which has been put aside in favor of the inkwell and map, accouterments of the staff officer. He is shown dictating to his aide in a setting that is probably imaginary.

FRANK BUCHSER, oil on canvas, 54 x 40¼, 1869
Lent by Kunstmuseum, Berne, Switzerland, Property of the Swiss Confederation

SITTING BULL *National Hero*   1834-1890

Sitting Bull, Sioux chief and medicine man, rallied his people and allies to defend their lands and preserve their ancient ways. Having tried diplomacy and found white men untrustworthy, he turned to war. As leader of the largest force of Western Plains Indians in history, estimated at from 2,500 to 4,000 braves, he sent his warriors against General George Custer at the Battle of the Little Big Horn in 1876. Sitting Bull did not join in the battle but remained in his camp "making medicine." Although Custer and his troops were slaughtered, the Indians later were driven into Canada. In 1881 the Sioux leader finally surrendered and

was forced to settle on the Standing Rock Reservation. There he remained bitterly unreconciled to the futility and starvation of reservation life. Ironically, he was killed by Indian police during an Indian disturbance in 1890.

Sitting Bull had a short, sturdy frame and a limp that was a reminder of his glorious days as a warrior. Although he was something of a visionary, his understanding of men and nature made him a shrewd leader. To the end he remained faithful to the Sioux ideals of generosity, courage, and tribal loyalty — qualities which he seldom found in white men.

D. F. BARRY, cabinet photograph, 11½ x 6⅞, 1885
Lent by the Library of Congress

ELIHU ROOT *International Lawyer*   **1845-1937**

Elihu Root believed that peace could be kept with legal and constitutional instruments. As Secretary of War (1899-1903) he solved, by these means, two of many problems arising out of the Spanish-American War. To soothe Filipinos rebelling against a transfer from Spanish to American dominion he drew up an organic act which protected individual liberty without granting independence. And to prevent newly independent Cuba from impairing its own sovereignty by making unwise agreements with other foreign powers he drafted the Platt Amendment to be attached to the Cuban constitution.

Root was a consistent advocate of arbitration and the rule of law in international affairs. He used his position as Theodore Roosevelt's Secretary of State (1905-1909) to negotiate arbitration treaties with twenty-four nations and to establish a Central American Court of Justice to adjudicate certain kinds of inter-American disputes. In 1910 he became a member of the Permanent Court of Arbitration at The Hague and president of the Carnegie Endowment for International Peace. He was awarded the Nobel Peace Prize in 1912.

After World War I Root favored American participation in an association of nations, but he found parts of the League of Nations Covenant unnecessarily rigid. Root, generally considered the chief architect of the World Court, was hopeful until 1934 that his own country would join it.

Wise and urbane, Root lacked the common touch of the politician, who must appeal to the people to secure office. His cause, the establishment of institutions for international justice, never captured the popular imagination. His years of service are remembered only by diplomatic historians and by humanitarians who dream of "what might have been."

AUGUSTUS VINCENT TACK, oil on canvas mounted on panel, 61⅛ x 49⅜, 1922
Gift of Duncan Phillips NPG.67.23

The
American
Is . . .

. . . a Rebel
and
Nonconformist

I would rather sit on a pumpkin and have it all to myself, than to be crowded on a velvet cushion.

Henry David Thoreau, *Walden* (1854)

The inalienable right to the pursuit of happiness proclaimed in the Declaration of Independence carries within it the right to be different. Although much has been said about American gregariousness and the pressures on the newly arrived immigrant to take on the national coloration of his chosen country, America has produced some notable loners and eccentrics and has coined the affectionate term "maverick" to describe them. Admiration for the gallant loser and the man who "stands up for what he thinks is right" has been a continuous thread in the pattern of American attitudes. Patriots of the American Revolution had no guillotine for Tories.

On the other hand, the rebel like John Brown who foments armed revolt cannot be tolerated even in a country born of revolution. And the Bill of Rights only protects the individual from interference from his government. A neighbor's sharp tongue and the ostracism a small town can inflict are penalties that the violator of convention must be prepared to face in any society.

HARRY WARNEKE, NEW YORK DAILY NEWS

CADWALLADER COLDEN   *Indomitable Tory*   1688-1776

There never was a more firm believer in the divine right of kings than Cadwallader Colden, Lieutenant Governor of New York from 1761 to 1775. An old and devoted servant of the Crown, his strict devotion to this institution did not allow him to yield to patriot pressure; in the tumultuous times before the Revolution he was irreconcilable to colonial cries for independence. He read the revolutionary tendency in America as a revolt against justified authority, and, alone and unsupported by public opinion, he fulfilled his duty of strictly enforcing the laws handed down by the Crown. Although the opportunity of peacemaking was his as a royal official, he persisted in loyalty to England and in oppression of the people; for trying to enforce the Stamp Act he was burned in effigy, and after the Battle of Lexington was forced into retirement.

Colden, however, was a colonial savant who displayed remarkable versatility. Although he began life in an uninspiring Scottish parish he had an outstanding career because of his keen sense of public duty and passion for discovery. His first publication, *The History of the Five Indian Nations Depending on the Province of New York* (1727), was considered an enlightened reference on the subject, and through his experimental work in botany, medicine, philosophy, and physics he became a prominent amateur scientist. If he had been less intransigent toward the colonists he would be remembered more for his accomplishments than for his failure.

MATTHEW PRATT, oil on canvas, 78½ x 47¼, 1772
Lent by New York Chamber of Commerce, New York, New York

AARON BURR   *Gentleman Adventurer*   **1756-1836**

There may be doubt that Aaron Burr was a rebel, but there is no question that he was a nonconformist, for his life fits no neat pattern. He was an officer in the Continental Army, a successful lawyer, a United States Senator, and Vice President — narrowly missing election to the Presidency. He killed Alexander Hamilton in a duel, was tried for treason and was acquitted, wandered abroad, returned to practice law, married at seventy-seven, and was divorced on the day of his death. Like the hero, or antihero, of a picaresque novel, he moved from one adventure to another, slipping into trouble — or success — slipping out, and wandering off to a new exploit.

Burr has never been a popular figure in American memory. He was too enigmatic to be neatly classified as either hero or villain. He lacked the dash and personal charm of a popular rogue-adventurer, and his shadowy "conspiracy" in the West, which seemed to threaten the existence of the nation, was too serious a matter to make him a Don Quixote. His career was not without effect, however. His electoral tie with Jefferson in 1800, from which he emerged as Vice President, led to the Twelfth Amendment, requiring candidates to run separately for the Presidency and Vice-Presidency. His trial of 1807, through Chief Justice John Marshall's decision, laid the basis for the federal courts' strict interpretation of treason.

JOHN VANDERLYN, oil on canvas, 28 x 21, not dated
Lent by Yale University Art Gallery, New Haven, Connecticut, Bequest of Oliver Burr Jennings

CHARLES BROCKDEN BROWN *Romanticist and Libertarian*   **1771-1810**

Charles Brockden Brown was the first American to make a profession of literature and the first American novelist to gain a European reputation. Possessing enormous intellectual energy, Brown attacked literature as he had the law and journalism, producing six novels in two years. In the process he suffered a characteristic American fate — he burned himself out before his time and wrote no more fiction.

In his short career and in his most notable works — *Wieland* (1798), *Edgar Huntly* (1799), and *Arthur Mervyn* (1799-1800) — Brown transplanted European Gothicism to American soil. His interest in somnambulism, ventriloquism, and spontaneous combustion and his exploration of Byronic character and the unconscious made him an influential precursor of Poe

and Hawthorne. Again, like James Fenimore Cooper after him, Brown emphasized the necessity of American subject matter, discovering terror among the villainous red men and wild animals of the forest rather than among Italian *banditti* and in haunted castles.

Brown believed in the perfectibility of man; one of the reasons he published as rapidly as he did was to propagate a moral vision. At one time or another he advocated equal rights for women, less constrictive divorce laws, better treatment of the working man, and decent treatment of the criminal. He was a freethinking libertarian in the best Romantic manner. If he has been forgotten as a reformer, as he has been forgotten as an artist, it is because his pioneering accomplishments were incorporated into those of other men.

WILLIAM DUNLAP, watercolor on ivory, 2¾ x 2¼, 1806
Lent by Mr. and Mrs. F. Woodson Hancock

OSCEOLA *Seminole Guerilla*   **about 1800-1838**

Although neither a hereditary nor an elected chief, Osceola was the defiant young leader of the Seminoles in their resistance to Indian emigration. He savagely plunged his great knife into the treaty he was asked to sign that would move his people from their beloved swamplands of the Southeast to the unoccupied territory west of the Mississippi. A mixture of hate and unconquerable resolution, his action at the signing of the peace treaty precipitated the Second Seminole War — a seven-year game of cat and mouse in the Florida swamps against federal troops.

Tricked into talking peace, Osceola was captured while carrying a white flag of truce and imprisoned in Fort Moultrie, South Carolina. George Catlin, painter of the American Indian, came to the prison and painted this portrait of Osceola, in full costume, shortly before he died of malaria. Catlin later wrote of the Seminole strong man's sensitive, almost effeminate countenance, which, when kindled by passion, glowed "with a hero's fire and lion's rage." Public opinion, inflamed by the treachery of Osceola's arrest and his "broken-hearted death in chains," turned him from villain into hero, from traitor into patriot.

GEORGE CATLIN, oil on canvas, mounted on aluminum, 30¾ x 25¾, about 1838
Lent by National Collection of Fine Arts, Smithsonian Institution

RALPH WALDO EMERSON *Apostle of Self-Reliance* **1803-1882**

Fifty years after the Revolution, Ralph Waldo Emerson established America's intellectual independence from Europe by giving the new nation its first native philosophy—transcendentalism. Emerson's philosophy was the spiritual equivalent of America's new confidence in her economic and political power. His thought had a strong impact on his contemporaries — Thoreau and Whitman particularly — and on later American intellectuals.

This noble sage from Concord, Massachusetts, de-clared the freedom of the soul and the revolt of the individual against society. In his essay on "Self-Reliance" (1841) Emerson wrote: "Society everywhere is in conspiracy against the manhood of every one of its members. . . . Whoso would be a man, must be a non-conformist." He placed his individual in communion with a transcendent universe but, unfortunately, this mystical side of his writings was often forgotten by industrialists and other self-made men who later used his expressions to justify their own materialism.

JEFFERSON DAVIS *Statesman of the "Lost Cause"* 1808-1889

"The man and the hour have met," proclaimed Robert Toombs when Jefferson Davis was inaugurated as President of the Confederate States of America. A lover of the Union and the Constitution, Davis was a most reluctant secessionist, hoping the South would remain a nation within the Union. But once the decision for secession was made he dedicated himself to the cause of independence, feeling that the South was fighting for the same cause as were the patriots of 1776.

Davis brought more experience to his Presidency than Abraham Lincoln did to his. A graduate of West Point, he had fought honorably in the Mexican War and had been nominated for brigadier general; he had served as United States Senator and later as Governor of Mississippi; and he had been an able Secretary of

War under Franklin Pierce. Yet Davis lacked the qualities of a great statesman. Unlike Lincoln he was not a practical politician. He was guided by righteous principle and patriotism, but his autocratic will often set the public and the administration in defiant opposition. He had courage and integrity, but he lacked tact and inner harmony.

The strain of office as President of the Confederacy told on his already weak body, as he suffered from nervous tension and a facial paralysis that partially blinded him. Imprisoned for two years after the war, he was indicted for treason but was never tried. He did not apply for a pardon and was thus ineligible to hold office again. He spent his last years on a plantation in Mississippi, writing *The Rise and Fall of the Confederate Government* (1881).

JOHN ELDER, oil on canvas, 30 x 25, not dated
Lent by The North Carolina Museum of Art, Raleigh, North Carolina

HENRY DAVID THOREAU *Adam in Babylon* 1817-1862

Henry David Thoreau had no job but many occupations. He was a naturalist, recording the facts of nature, the depth of ice, the day lily's blossom. A transcendentalist, for whom the facts themselves blossomed into truths beneath the pressure of the imagination. A revolutionary — the first in America to speak publicly on behalf of John Brown — and a dissident, who was jailed for refusing to pay his poll tax in protest against slavery.

He was also linguist and scholar, learned in Greek, Latin, Italian, French, German, and Spanish and familiar with Oriental classics in translation. A teacher, who innovated in America the use of field trips to study nature. A wit, who in answer to a deathbed question, "Are you ready to make your peace with God?" replied (or so it has been reported), "I did not know we had quarreled." An editor, who took his turn at the famous transcendentalist magazine *The Dial*. An inventor—of a graphite pencil which bettered his family's business — handyman, carpenter, and painter. An excursionist who traveled several times to Cape Cod, Maine, and New York; to Canada and Minnesota; and for *A Week on the Concord and Merrimack Rivers* (1849).

Most of all, of course, Thoreau was a stylist and author who went to the woods "to live deliberately, to front only the essential facts of life, and see if I could not learn what it had to teach." His residence at Walden auspiciously began on Independence Day 1845 and ended a little more than two years later. But as Thoreau tells it in his most famous work, *Walden* (1854), the experiment ended with the death of winter and the onset of spring — with that part of seasonal rejuvenation around which a wise man could learn to live his life.

BENJAMIN D. MAXHAM, daguerreotype, 2 x 1½, 1856
Lent by The Thoreau Society and the Concord Free Public Library, Concord, Massachusetts

KENNEDY GALLERIES, INC.

ALBERT PINKHAM RYDER   *Painter of the Inner Life*   **1847-1917**

A largely self-taught artist whose unique style expresses a visionary world, Albert Pinkham Ryder remained a dedicated solitary in his New York bachelor studio for over ten years. He would brood for years over a small picture, deeply absorbed in his work and never entirely satisfied with what he had done. His total output numbered only about 150 works.

Experiencing the dream world and natural world as one, Ryder achieved a subjectivity and purity of image that set him apart and gave his paintings an intense, haunting reality. In seeking this intenser reality he persisted in a technique of overpainting and glazing that has caused many of his works to deteriorate disastrously. He devoted many of his last years to restoring his decaying works; but he once remarked to the artist Salvator Guarino, "When a thing has the elements of beauty from the beginning it cannot be destroyed."

Ryder's art, remote from the current naturalistic spirit of the Hudson River School and of genre painting, was highly individual — anticipating the abstract naturalism of Marsden Hartley, Georgia O'Keefe, and Milton Avery. In a letter to a friend he gives the best available description of his search for symbolic meaning in nature and literary myth:

Have you ever seen an inch worm crawl up a leaf or twig, and then clinging to the very end revolve in the air, feeling for something to reach something?
That's like me. I am trying to find something out there beyond the place on which I have a footing.

SELF-PORTRAIT, oil on cigar-box top, 6 x 4½, before 1881
Lent by a private collection

EUGENE V. DEBS   *Prisoner of Principle*

1855-1926

"Stand by your principles, regardless of consequences" was the advice that Daniel and Marguerite Debs wired to their son Eugene Debs on the day the bitter Pullman strike of 1894 collapsed. And this was the advice that Eugene Debs followed throughout his life, whether he was leading railroad workers on strike, arguing against American participation in World War I, or advocating socialism to workers and farmers that massed to hear his inflammatory speeches.

Beginning his career as an organizer for the Brotherhood of Locomotive Firemen, Debs became president of the American Railway Union, an "industrial" union involving all who worked in any capacity in the railroad industry. His painful experiences in strikes against the Great Northern Railroad and the Pullman

Company and his imprisonment under the pro-business administration of President Cleveland converted him to socialism. He remained a firm believer in that philosophy for the rest of his life.

As a Socialist, Debs ran for the Presidency five times — in 1900, 1904, 1908, 1912, and 1920. Once he conducted his campaign from behind the walls of the federal penitentiary in Atlanta, where he was serving a sentence for speaking out against prosecution of persons charged with sedition during World War I. In 1912 he polled nearly a million votes.

Debs once summed up his philosophy: "While there is a lower class, I am in it; while there is a criminal element, I am of it; while there is a soul in prison, I am not free."

Louis Mayer, bronze, 25¾ high, 1919
NPG.68.36

106

H. L. MENCKEN *Scornful Educator*   1880-1956

H. L. Mencken can be called America's greatest master of invective and vituperation. Criticism was his trade, but name-calling was his trademark. He wrote six volumes frankly entitled *Prejudices*, and he invented some enduring terms for his fellow citizens. Americans whom he scorned he called the "booboisie"; the rural folk he encountered during the Scopes monkey trial he called "gaping primates" from the "Bible belt."

Mencken despised the conventional moralism of American life — with its hypocritical codes and persistent Puritanism — and he savagely denounced the democratic process because he believed it led to "the worship of jackals by jackasses." He was against mindless American patriotism "because it demands the acceptance of propositions that are obviously imbecile — *e.g.* that an American Presbyterian is the equal of Anatole France, Brahms, or Ludendorff." Although he mistrusted the common man — and some

have seen in that mistrust an incipient fascism — he stood against censorship and interference with personal freedom. Like Whitman, he gloried in his contradictions.

Impelled by the necessity of reforming American taste, Mencken championed such new and relatively iconoclastic writers as Theodore Dreiser and Sinclair Lewis, but his ultimate claim to our attention is his championing of American English. Most surprisingly for a journalist who scorned the academy and its residents, Mencken produced a monumental work of genuine scholarly analysis. Entitled *The American Language* (1919), it is an attempt to define the Americanness of English — its origin, growth, present condition, and future development; its pronunciation, spelling, and slang — and remains his finest effort toward the education of his countrymen.

Nikol Schattenstein, oil on canvas, 40⅛ x 30, 1927
Lent by The Enoch Pratt Free Library, Baltimore, Maryland

The
American
Is . . .

. . . Practical

Pragmatism is willing to take anything, to follow either
logic or the senses and to count . . . mystical experiences
if they have practical consequences. Her only test
of probable truth is what works best . . . .

William James, *Pragmatism, A New Name for*
Some Old Ways of Thinking (1907)

"Will it work?" is the criterion which the American ap-
plies to his ideas as well as his implements. He has adapted
old tools to new uses — to survive in the forest, then on
the prairie, and finally on the plains — and he has been
ingenious in finding new mechanical ways to do things
once done by hand. Since he had little time for reading
abstruse works on politics, his governmental institutions
were devised through trial and error rather than according
to a preconceived system. Practical by nature and in their
everyday lives, Americans also have been the philosophers
of the practical: Henry George in economics, William
James and Charles S. Peirce in psychology and ethics, and
John Dewey in aesthetics and education applied the principles of pragmatism to large areas of human knowledge.

In this country, people — like tools and ideas — are
judged by how well they work. The American's parents
and mentors never tire of telling him "Anything worth

doing is worth doing well," and by "worth doing" they mean useful. From the time Captain John Smith declared that a "plaine souldier that can use a pickaxe and a spade is better than five knights" society has scorned the dilettante who violates the gospel of work. Idleness was considered a sin not only by the Puritan but by the unchurched, swearing frontier farmer, who needed all his sons' energies to get in a crop, and by the Catholic Irish or Italian factory worker whose income would not feed his family unless several of its members were breadwinners.

Practicality has been the enemy of artistic and often of intellectual activity in America. Until a sophisticated technology began to make a college education the shortest route to a good job or profession, a youth's education was often terminated early so that "he could get down to something useful." Perhaps the crisis faced by the American of the 1960s is partly owing to his difficulty in adjusting to a world in which his technology threatens to make his usefulness obsolete.

Amateurs
and
Versatilists

The American historically is a nonspecialist — a Jack-of-many-trades, if often master of none. His versatility is born partly of genteel tradition and partly of harsh necessity. Blessed with leisure and wealth and obliged by isolation to devise its own entertainment, the eighteenth-century English gentry cultivated virtuosity and amateurism. The typical country gentleman, whether of Kent or Virginia, was an accomplished farmer, hunter, horseman, breeder of wild and domestic animals, and often a collector and connoisseur; his wife and daughters were skilled amateurs of the gentle arts — music, painting, sewing, and the French language.

The early pioneer settler, on the other hand, confronted by a continent vast in resources and free of customs, was at liberty — and indeed was forced — to learn many skills and crafts. Frequently remote from established communities with their specialized trades and professions, the frontiersman had to be not only farmer, hunter, and warrior but also carpenter, smith, and tanner. To survive in a primitive, unfamiliar, and unpredictable environment and to advance his fortunes, he became highly self-sufficient and adaptable. What he lacked in specialized skills he supplied with specialized tools. And like the more affluent plantation owner, he learned to provide his own recreation. Today the American is a Sunday hobbyist by choice.

A profusion of opportunities and the absence of professional or governmental requirements challenged the American to try himself at a variety of careers. An apostle of self-education and self-advancement, he came to believe firmly in learning by earning. Hence he moved easily between land and sea, farm and factory, relying on his flexibility and versatility to cultivate the "main chance." His success, as an individual and a nation, have led him to admire his kind — the versatile amateur who becomes so proficient that he is recognized and rewarded as a professional — and, frequently, to distrust the expert. Only as society became more complex in organization did the American begin to respect the rights of labor and to value the specialist. Nevertheless, he continues to find satisfaction in his ability to "do it himself."

BENJAMIN FRANKLIN *Renaissance Man* 1706-1790

"B. Franklin, Printer" — as he still described himself after he had become an international figure — was an extraordinary combination of shrewdness, wit, curiosity, earthiness, formidable talents, and ingenuity: in brief, a genius. His career is a classic American success story. Of humble origins, he played brilliantly every role that opportunity offered him. His printing business was so lucrative that he retired from it at forty-two. His interest in improving the community of Philadelphia led him to help establish a city hospital, police force, and fire brigade. His pursuit of knowledge for its own sake inspired him to found America's first circulating library, the American Philosophical Society(1743), and an academy for youth(1753) that was to become the University of Pennsylvania.

Public office sought him. He served at the Albany Congress of 1754, where his plan to unite the colonies was adopted in preference to others; at the Second Continental Congress in 1776; and at the Constitutional Convention in 1787. During the Revolution he was United States ambassador to France, where his unpretentious, democratic bearing made him the idol of the French people.

Science, however, was this versatile man's abiding interest. He invented the so-called "Franklin stove," and an ingenious musical instrument called an armonica for which Mozart and Beethoven composed. He studied the Gulf Stream, the effects of cooling by evaporation, the character of a whirlwind, and the causes of nor'easters and the common cold. The discoverer of the lightning rod, he wrote regarding his research on electricity:

On further experiment . . . I have observed a phenomenon or two that I cannot at present account for . . . and am therefore become a little diffident of my hypothesis and ashamed that I expressed myself in so positive a manner. . . . If there is no other use discovered of electricity, this however is something considerable, that it may serve to make a vain man humble.

MASON CHAMBERLIN, oil on canvas, 49 x 39, 1762
Lent by the Philadelphia Museum of Art, Gift of Mr. and Mrs. Wharton Sinkler

PAUL REVERE *Patriot Craftsman*

1735-1818

Paul Revere is remembered in American history for his famous ride to Lexington on 18 April 1775 — a journey undertaken to warn John Hancock and Samuel Adams that British troops were coming. This was not the only ride that Paul Revere made in defense of American independence, however, for he was deeply involved in revolutionary activity. A member of the Committee of Correspondence and of the Sons of Liberty, he was also the organizer of the first American intelligence network and the official courier for the Massachusetts Provincial Assembly to the Continental Congress.

While he did not receive a command in the Revolutionary Army, Revere used his talents in other ways to aid the patriots. He designed and built a mill at Canton, Massachusetts, in order to supply the soldiers with gunpowder. He devised the first official seal for

the colonies; and he designed and printed the first issue of Continental currency. After the war he mastered the difficult art of bell-casting and discovered a process for rolling sheet copper for shipbuilding. Some of his rolled copper found its way to construction of the boiler for Robert Fulton's steamboat.

A warm, generous man, Revere spent long hours in church and civic activities in addition to those devoted to responsibilities as the father of eight children. He persisted in wearing Revolutionary costumes long after they were out of fashion in order to express his patriotic devotion to his country and to the cause of freedom. Considered the best silversmith of his time, Revere is shown in this portrait holding a silver teapot — a superb example of his excellent workmanship — that awaits decorative tooling.

JOHN SINGLETON COPLEY, oil on canvas, 35 x 28½, about 1769
Lent by Museum of Fine Arts, Boston, Gift of Joseph W., William B., and Edward H. R. Revere

CHARLES WILLSON PEALE *Virtuoso of the Young Republic* **1741-1827**

Charles Willson Peale was an innocent enthusiast, supremely confident of the importance of every project he undertook. He was successively — and sometimes simultaneously — a saddler, clockmaker, silversmith, portrait painter, patriot soldier, and naturalist. After studying under John Singleton Copley and Benjamin West he became self-appointed portrait painter to the Continental Congress at Philadelphia in 1776.

Peale's most enduring interest, however, developed after the Revolution when he discovered the Enlightenment and natural history. Having painted miniatures of General Washington and other eminent Americans during encampments with the Revolutionary Army, he determined to enlarge his portrait gallery into a museum, where art and science would be combined into a "world in miniature." Accordingly he collected such natural wonders as a five-legged cow and the skeleton of a mastodon which, with his portraits, he exhibited first in his own home in Philadelphia and later at the American Philosophical Society and Independence Hall. His museum became the most notable of his day.

The self-portrait shown here was painted when Peale was in his early sixties. At one time hopeful of living to be two hundred, Peale was proud of his enduring youthfulness, which he celebrates in this likeness. A year later he acknowledged that in order to paint he needed those glasses which here he has thrust triumphantly back from his face. He died at the age of eighty-six.

Peale's Philadelphia Museum did not survive long after his death. More enduring were his forthright paintings — and those of a large and gifted family, distinguished painters and naturalists in their own right — as well as another project, the Pennsylvania Academy of Fine Arts (1805).

SELF-PORTRAIT, oil on canvas, 26 x 22, about 1804
Lent by The Pennsylvania Academy of the Fine Arts, Philadelphia, Pennsylvania

ROYALL TYLER *First Yankee on Olympus*   **1757-1826**

Royall Tyler was equally successful at law and literature. His legal career brought him local repute in
Boston and then in Vermont, where he served as chief
justice of the state's supreme court (1807-1813) and
where in 1802 he rendered the decision that slaves
could not be brought into Vermont territory. His
literary avocation brought him international acclaim
for his satiric novel *The Algerine Captive* (1797) and
for *The Contrast* (1787), the first comedy written by
a native American and produced by a professional
company. Declaring America's literary independence
in these works, Tyler urged that his countrymen no
longer depend on the literature of England but rather
that "we write our own books of amusement and that
they exhibit our own manners." Of less literary importance but of equal charm was his long reflective
poem "The Chestnut Tree" written two years before
his death but not published until 1931.

UNIDENTIFIED ARTIST, watercolor on ivory, 2 x 1½, not dated
Lent by The Honorable William R. Tyler

DeWITT CLINTON *Great Apollo*   **1769-1828**

DeWitt Clinton, a man of democratic principles and aristocratic tastes, was statesman, reformer, and savant. Devoting his life to public service, Clinton also found time for scholarly study and promoted scientific farming. As the mayor of New York City for more than ten years and as the Governor of the state for all but one year between 1817 and 1828, he was responsible for the establishment of public schools, asylums, and hospitals, for stronger police and military protection, for improvement in the condition of the disadvantaged, and for the construction of a canal to connect Lake Erie with the Hudson River and the Atlantic Ocean. Labeled the "father of the spoils system," Clinton also supported states rights, a wide program of internal improvement, and a plan for the abolition of slavery; his administrative competence carried many of his liberal ideas into practice. His political career was marred only by his failure to win election to the Presidency in 1812, when he was roundly defeated by James Madison.

Clinton was a cultured man, not unlike Thomas Jefferson. He was the second president of the American Academy of Art, the founder of the New-York Historical Society, and an active member of many scientific and literary societies. An accomplished naturalist, he published important papers in botany, geology, and agronomy. He also conducted research of the Great Lakes and on the Indians. Although he was overbearing and personally unengaging, Clinton was a person of vision, tenacity, and integrity. His physical appearance was so impressive that he was called "Magnus Apollo."

JOHN WESLEY JARVIS, oil on canvas, 48¼ x 36⅜, not dated
Gift of Andrew Mellon   *NPG.42.12*

EDWARD HICKS *Pious Primitive*

1780-1849

As a primitive painter, Edward Hicks spoke for the earnest piety of rural America in the early 1800s. A minister in the Society of Friends, his paintings expressed the Quaker ideal of peace and the country dweller's love of land. His religion was his passion; painting mostly biblical scenes, "he taught the gospel with his paint brush." In this portrait by his cousin and pupil, Thomas Hicks, he is shown working on "The Peaceable Kingdom" which illustrates the prophecy, in the book of *Isaiah*, of the lion lying down with the lamb. He painted over a hundred variations of this subject, often printing the scriptural text on the canvas.

Although Hicks was a successful sign and carriage painter, his self-taught art sprang from his inner life rather than his craft. His trade, however, helped him to fulfill his belief that the ministry should be self-sustaining. Caring only for that which was useful, he fondly regarded his canvases as "vain daubing," but the profits they brought justified them as a necessary occupation. His great ability at lettering also led him to launch a side industry of making alphabet blocks for children, a not-too-successful business but one he took seriously. "Humble industry" was to Hicks the basis of reverence, and although he often longed to become an itinerant preacher his obsession with religious pragmatism would not allow him to follow that vocation.

THOMAS HICKS, oil on canvas, 27 x 22, not dated
Lent by Abby Aldrich Rockefeller Folk Art Collection, Williamsburg, Virginia

SAMUEL F. B. MORSE   *Artist-Engineer*   **1791-1872**

Portraiture and politics, photography and journalism, telegraphy and teaching — the gifted Samuel F. B. Morse might have pursued a dozen careers in a country where there was a market for every practical vocation.

A skillful organizer, Morse founded the National Academy of Design (1826) and the New York *Journal of Commerce* (1827). He was a gifted portraitist, a teacher of painting and design at New York University, and the first professor of fine arts in an American academic institution. He ran for mayor of New York and for Congress on the Nativist platform. He

taught Mathew Brady to use Daguerre's "magic box" and thus can be credited with introducing photography to America. Although he was not alone in early research on telegraphy, Morse's contribution and the code he devised for sending messages by telegraph made possible a great communications industry which he helped stretch across the Atlantic.

Yet Samuel Morse considered himself a failure. He wanted above all to paint sublime historical and allegorical pictures at a time when most Americans were too occupied with practical affairs to feel a need for aesthetic pleasures.

SELF-PORTRAIT, oil on canvas, 30 x 25, about 1814
Lent by Addison Gallery of American Art, Andover, Massachusetts

WILLIAM CULLEN BRYANT   *City Editor and Country Poet*   **1794-1878**

William Cullen Bryant is remembered as a poet of rural New England and an early member of the Romantic literary movement in this country. To his contemporaries, however, he was better known as editor-in-chief of one of the country's leading reform newspapers, the New York *Evening Post*. His dual career symbolizes an America emerging from a rural, regional simplicity into a complex society with grave national concerns.

Bryant entered the world of journalism by accident. Dissatisfied with law and unable to support his family as a poet, he assumed a temporary position on the *Evening Post* in 1826. Within three years he was editor, a position he held for nearly half a century. By 1840 his role as defender of the national interests had earned him recognition as a leading Democratic editor, although his opposition to slavery led him to support the Republicans and Lincoln's campaign for the Presidency in 1860. Because he insisted that newspaper writing be both precise and accurate, Bryant played an important part in elevating the literary style and moral tone of modern journalism.

William Cullen Bryant was a man of deep reserve. In spite of his strong commitment to social and political causes he found the solitude of nature more in harmony with his reflective mind; he wrote poetry to communicate his intense love of natural beauty. In his own day he was greatly praised for his long philosophical "Thanatopsis" (1817) and blank verse translations of Homer, but his poetic reputation rests today on a handful of reflective nature lyrics — notably, "To a Waterfowl" and "To the Fringed Gentian." Walt Whitman called Bryant "bard of the river and wood."

FRANK BUCHSER, oil on canvas, 54 x 40¼, 1868
Lent by Kunstmuseum, Basel, Switzerland

Inventors
and
Innovators

"New" to the American has usually been synonymous with "better." His dedication to the "new" reflects not just a fascination with the novel and strange — although that too is in his makeup — but chiefly an impatience with old devices and procedures if more efficient ones can be developed. A strange physical environment, so different from that of Europe, demanded invention and innovation: Broad fields in place of intensively farmed plots stimulated the invention of the reaper and barbed wire; great distances between settlements produced the circuit rider and eventually the development of more efficient means of transportation. Moreover, intermingling cultures adopted each other's ways: Englishmen learned from Indians along the Atlantic coast how to plant corn, whereas Plains Indians were introduced to horses by Spaniards.

The American's preoccupation with being up to date is also part of his fresh openmindedness and commitment to the possibility of progress. But his optimism has also blinded him both to the meretricious in the newfangled and to much that is valuable in his heritage. He has replaced distinguished old buildings with new ones whose ugliness is tolerated because, presumably, they are more functional; he has destroyed natural beauty to make way for the superhighway; and he has polluted air and water in the name of industrial efficiency. Now that the American is learning how necessary cultural roots, scenic beauty, and clean air are to human health and happiness his innovations often take the form of restoration and repair.

BENJAMIN RUSH   *Physician to the People*   1745-1813

After graduating from the College of New Jersey (Princeton University) and completing his medical education at the University of Edinburgh, Benjamin Rush in 1769 returned to his native city of Philadelphia to practice and teach medicine. He became the most distinguished physician of his time. He published the first American chemistry text in 1770, and later he established the first free medical clinic in America. In 1783 he had joined the staff of the Pennsylvania Hospital where he served until his death. After the University of Pennsylvania was founded in 1791 Rush became a professor of medicine and clinical practice in its medical school.

Rush's career was divided between dogged credulity and courageous action. He developed a new "system" of practical medicine which — somewhat ingenuously — reduced all diseases to a spasm in the blood vessels and all treatment to "depletion" or bloodletting. During Philadelphia's terrible yellow fever epidemic in 1793 Rush worked heroically and — after most of his colleagues had fled — courageously remained behind when the disease returned to the city in 1798. To the consternation of his colleagues he persisted in treating victims of the epidemic with his "system."

Rush had had an equally active and significant career as a patriot. Numbering John Adams and Thomas Jefferson among his intimate friends, he sat in the Continental Congress, signed the Declaration of Independence, and later served in the Pennsylvania convention which ratified the Federal Constitution. His brief career as a surgeon general of the Revolutionary Army had ended abruptly after he was involved in a conspiracy to remove George Washington as commanding general. In the last dozen years of his life, however, he returned to public service as treasurer of the United States Mint.

An active social reformer, Rush helped organize the Pennsylvania antislavery society, opposed capital punishment, and agitated for prison reform, the education of women, and the study of veterinary medicine. Some have claimed that because of his pioneer work in experimental physiology and his contributions on mental disease he deserves the title of "father of American psychiatry." The temperance movement is unanimous in recognizing him as a founder.

THOMAS SULLY, oil on canvas, 42½ x 33½, 1812
Lent by Mr. and Mrs. Benjamin Rush

ROBERT FULTON *American Daedalus* **1765-1815**

Men had been exploring the idea of the steamship for twenty years before Robert Fulton was born and for thirty years before James Watt developed the engine with which the idea could be made a reality. Several Frenchmen, the Americans John Fitch and James Rumsey, and the Englishman William Symington all had operated technically successful vessels driven by steam power before Fulton had. Yet Fulton's was the one that counted. When his "North River steam boat" (later named the *Clermont*) chugged up the Hudson River in 1807 it was not just a technical success but a commercial success as well. Fulton's achievement was to build a steamboat that worked both well and profitably, a combination that Americans have always been quick to appreciate.

Fulton's ventures extended far beyond his interest in steamboats. He left his native Pennsylvania at twenty-one to study painting in Europe. By 1796, when he began calling himself a "civil engineer," he was absorbed in the whole range of technical problems involved in water transport. He devised an effective canal-dredging machine, cast-iron aqueducts, and a small, working submarine—the *Nautilus*—in which he tried to interest both the French and British during the Napoleonic wars.

Like most successful inventors Fulton was not an unlettered tinkerer. He was well read in physical science and applied its principles intelligently to achieve practical benefits.

BENJAMIN WEST, oil on canvas, 36 x 28, 1806
Lent by New York State Historical Association, Cooperstown, New York

ELI WHITNEY *Yankee Wizard*

1765-1825

If there is a single historical figure whose name instantly evokes a pious image of Yankee ingenuity it must surely be Eli Whitney of Connecticut. Morse's portrait, shown here, conveys something of Whitney's shrewdness and calculation and hints at a quality of flinty determination associated with New Englanders.

Whitney invented the cotton gin in 1793. By providing an economical way of separating the short-staple cotton boll from its tenacious seed, Whitney helped make cotton the nation's chief raw material export, and thus the chief source of investment capital for the country's rapidly expanding industry. Ironi-

cally, Whitney's invention had unfortunate consequences both for him and the nation. He personally realized little profit from his machine; and the institution of slavery, which had seemed doomed to extinction, acquired new vitality following its wide use.

The gin alone would have established Whitney as an important figure in the history of technology, but he is also usually credited with developing the system of interchangeable parts. He perfected this system — later so important to mass production — while manufacturing firearms for the federal government.

SAMUEL F. B. MORSE, oil on canvas, 35½ x 27⅝, not dated
Lent by Yale University Art Gallery, New Haven, Connecticut

BENJAMIN SILLIMAN *Senior Scientist* 1779-1864

Benjamin Silliman was one of the most prominent and influential men of science in America in the first half of the nineteenth century. An exceptionally gifted teacher and a prolific writer rather than an original researcher, Silliman established science on an equal basis with other academic subjects and made the deeply religious nation conscious of its value. Silliman's utilitarian rather than speculative mind looked upon science as a means of promoting human comfort and happiness.

As professor of chemistry, natural history, and geology at Yale University, Silliman had a profound effect on higher education. Helping to establish the Yale Medical School and what was to become the Sheffield Scientific School, he is credited with establishing in this country graduate education leading to advanced degrees. In the classroom at Yale, where he presented his material with great clarity and elegance, he accompanied his lectures with ingenious experiments. Silliman gathered around him a group of assistants who were to become the leaders of American science and education in the following generation. He lectured widely to the public in New York and various New England states to advance science. A founder and first editor of the *American Journal of Science and Arts* (1818), Silliman contributed numerous articles to this and other publications and he wrote several texts on chemistry and geology.

A deeply religious man, Silliman felt that the study of science enabled man to understand the manifestation of God in the world and that it was man's duty to interpret God's work reverently.

JOHN TRUMBULL, oil on panel, 19¼ x 15⅝, not dated
Gift of Alice Silliman Hawkes   NPG.68.6

EDGAR ALLAN POE *Dark Angel of American Letters* **1809-1849**

"The world shall be my theater," wrote the young Edgar Allan Poe hopefully. The hope was not fulfilled in his lifetime. Poverty, family quarrels, alcoholism, gambling, and what an unsophisticated age called "melancholy" destroyed him at forty, before the world could fully appreciate his genius. His popular reputation rests upon a handful of horror stories — "tales of the grotesque" Poe called them — and a few poems, notably "The Raven" and "Annabel Lee." Nor have the literary historians, who find his dark, brooding fantasies alternately inept and profound, succeeded in fixing his place.

Few have denied, nevertheless, Poe's literary originality and inventiveness. Through prosodic innovation and haunting symbols he achieved in "The City in the Sea," "Israfel," and other major poems a new poetic voice. In "The Murders in the Rue Morgue" he originated the "detective" story in English, and in his character Dupin he gave the world the first of a long line of fictional criminologists. His critical writings were among the best and most caustic of his day, while his outstanding editorial work for the *Southern Literary Messenger* helped to create the South's tradition of letters. In macabre stories like "The Fall of the House of Usher" and "The Masque of the Red Death," and especially in his hypnotic verse and the posthumously published *Marginalia,* he anticipated Baudelaire and the French Symbolists, upon whom he exerted a strong influence.

Poe's preoccupation with the "terror of the soul" — with probing the edge of the unconscious — did not find an audience in America until a few years before his death. In time, however, the world did become his theater, for he was the first American writer not only to earn an international reputation but to exert an international influence.

W. S. Hartshorn, daguerreotype, 3⅛ x 2⅝, 1848
Lent by the American Antiquarian Society, Worcester, Massachusetts

MATHEW B. BRADY   *Pioneer Historian*   **about 1823-1896**

"From the first, I regarded myself as under obligation to my country to preserve the faces of its historical men and women," Mathew Brady stated in explanation of his pictorial essays. In the process of preserving the American scene in photography he captured some of the brightest and darkest hours of this country's history. He worked diligently to master the infant art of photography, and he was usually the first to experiment with technical innovations. After he had discarded the daguerreotype for the wet-plate process his pictures became superior to all that had been made before. "Photograph by Brady" became the best known by-line of his generation. There were few celebrities of the day who did not visit his fashionable studios in New York and Washington. Abraham

Lincoln once said that Brady's photographs of him helped make him President. Brady's *Gallery of Illustrious Americans*, depicting for posterity notables of the day, was published in 1850.

It is for his photographic documentation of the Civil War, however, that Brady is chiefly remembered. Wearing a linen duster and straw hat, he traveled with his assistants in his famed "What-is-it?" wagon to almost every theater of the war. Ironically, the war which made him famous also destroyed him. Nearly blind from his exhausting work and destitute after using all his money to finance expeditions to the battlefronts, Brady never regained his early prestige. His last years were spent in poverty, his efforts remaining unappreciated until long after his death.

CHARLES LORING ELLIOTT, oil on canvas, 24 x 20, not dated
Lent by The Metropolitan Museum of Art, Gift of the Friends of Mathew Brady, 1896

HENRY GEORGE *Social Prophet* 1839-1897

More important for his influence on others than for any actual events in his own life, Henry George was the author of *Progress and Poverty* (1879), a graphic indictment of the paradoxical increase of wealth and want in industrial America. Himself a victim of abject poverty for years, he proposed by way of solving America's economic ills a "single tax" — a tax on land that would eliminate all other forms of economic rent and taxation. Although few accepted his solution, George's book generated a chain of ideas that began with "progressivism" late in the nineteenth century and that culminated in the "New Deal" in the 1930s.

His proposals helped stimulate the powerful political reform movement represented on the municipal level by Tom Johnson in Cleveland, on the state level by Senator Robert La Follette of Wisconsin, and on the national level by Theodore Roosevelt.

In 1886 a new party composed of labor leaders and middle-class reformers nominated Henry George for mayor of New York. Although defeated by the Tammany candidate, he polled more votes than Theodore Roosevelt who ran for the same office. In the midst of another strenuous campaign for the New York mayoralty he succumbed suddenly to apoplexy.

GEORGE DE FOREST BRUSH, oil on panel, 8⅝ x 7⅞, not dated
NPG.67.53

126

WILLIAM JAMES   *Mediator between Two Cultures*   1842-1910

William James, Harvard professor of physiology, psychology, and philosophy, was a "sort of Irishman among the Brahmins" according to his colleague George Santayana. Although remembered less today than his novelist brother Henry, he left a larger mark on the social thought of his own time — and ours.

After an irregular education under the direction of his eccentric father, William James started out to be an artist but soon abandoned the studio for the laboratory and Harvard Medical School, where he took a degree in 1868. As a medical student, and from Louis Agassiz whom he accompanied on an expedition to the Amazon, he learned a lifelong respect for facts and direct observation. A frail constitution and chronic nervous depression prevented him from continuing his career in medicine, but in 1872 he accepted an instructorship in physiology in Harvard College — the first of a long succession of posts at that institution.

Bringing his knowledge of physiology to bear on the new social science of psychology, James taught a celebrated course relating the two disciplines. In 1875 he established the first psychology laboratory in America and in 1878 began work on his monumental *Principles of Psychology* (1890), which in an abridged edition became the most popular textbook on the subject in this country. Among other innovational achievements, James — as much as John Dewey — opened the way to modern child-centered educational theory.

After 1890 James gradually shifted his teaching and writing from psychology to philosophy. Sensitive to the claims of both faith and science, he sought to make them complementary rather than conflicting by reconciling the concepts of a righteous God and freedom of the will with the scientific temper. His ideas were presented in a series of major works culminating in his famous *Pragmatism* (1907). William James is recognized as the principal proponent of American pragmatism — the philosophical doctrine that judges the truth of an idea or event by its consequences. Possessing a humorous, warm, open nature, he devised a philosophical system that stresses the actual appearances of things and satisfies the human need for individualism and freedom. In doing so he anticipated the direction taken by the generation that followed him.

ELLEN EMMET RAND, oil on canvas, 54½ x 41¾, 1910
Lent by Fogg Art Museum, Cambridge, Massachusetts

LOUIS H. SULLIVAN   *Philosopher of Steel and Concrete*   **1856-1924**

Louis H. Sullivan was a principal founder of modern architecture. His dictum that "form follows function" — emphasizing the organic relationship between the outward design of a structure and its inner purpose — had a profound and pervasive influence upon modern design. His Wainwright Building (1890-1891) in St. Louis was the architectural forerunner of the twentieth-century skyscraper, while the decorative features of his Auditorium Building (1886-1890) and the present Carson Pirie Scott Building (1899) — both in Chicago — anticipated modern, organic ornamentation.

Sullivan's importance, however, lies more in his seminal ideas than in his buildings, for, like many artistic innovators, he found few appreciative clients. His architectural "functionalism" was part of a larger philosophy. Regarding architecture as the most social

of the arts, he rejected classical and Gothic styles as unsuitable for expressing the spirit of modern civilization. What he sought — and ultimately inspired — were new forms of design based on the amazing achievements of modern technology. Above all, he sought an architecture that would reflect the character and aspirations of American democracy. What the poet Walt Whitman had celebrated in words the architectural poet Sullivan wished to celebrate in stone, steel, and concrete.

Through the "Chicago School" of architects, of which he was the leader and theoretician, and through Frank Lloyd Wright, his greatest disciple, Sullivan has left an enduring mark on the American landscape and skyline.

FRANK A. WERNER, oil on canvas, 63⅛ x 41⅛, 1918
Lent by Chicago Historical Society, Chicago, Illinois,
Gift of Chicago Chapter, American Institute of Architects

JOHN DEWEY *Practical Cogitator*   **1859-1952**

John Dewey was born in Vermont the same year Darwin's *Origin of Species* was published. He thus began his long career at a time when evolutionary ideas were having a pronounced impact on philosophy and education and when the concept of biological organisms adapting to environment overshadowed all other hypotheses. Strongly influenced by William James's pragmatism, Dewey held that truth was relative, empirical, and evolutionary. He lived to see his insistence on the direct relation between learning and experience widely incorporated into the educational theories and practices of many nations, including his own.

Dewey taught at the University of Chicago during its first decade and at Columbia University from 1904 until his retirement in 1930. He was a founder of the American Association of University Professors and of the American Civil Liberties Union. No occupant of an ivory tower, Dewey's deep sense of commitment to life led him to take stands on virtually every controversial social issue that occurred during the long span of his working career.

He was a wretched lecturer ("damnable," James said), but by some curious alchemy his students remembered him as an inspired teacher. His numerous publications were wide ranging — from psychology and logic to aesthetics and education. By the time of his death, at ninety-three, the excesses of progressive education — especially the theory of "life adjustment" fashionable in the 1940s — were being roundly denounced as pernicious in many quarters. Nevertheless, Dewey often served as a scapegoat for people who had never understood — or read — him.

JACOB EPSTEIN, bronze, 13 high, not dated
Lent by Mrs. John Dewey, Courtesy of Teachers College, Columbia University, New York, New York

ADOLF MEYER *Dean of American Psychiatry* **1866-1950**

As a son of a Protestant reform minister in Switzerland, Adolf Meyer grew up in an atmosphere of liberalism and reflection. He learned to respect human dignity and to speculate about the relationship of mind and body. These concerns guided him during his professional training as a medical student in Germany; during postgraduate study in Paris, Edinburgh, and London; and in his neuroanatomical research in America, to which he came in 1892. He ultimately developed his school of "psychobiology," which greatly advanced psychiatry by bringing together separate branches of medicine into a study of man as an integrated whole.

Meyer humanized the approach to mental illness by stressing the use of "critical common sense," rejecting earlier rigid theories, and introducing improvements in the management of mental institutions. He was a pioneer in the mental hygiene movement, which linked psychology and sociology, and a forceful participant in many other causes to benefit mankind. His most notable work, however, was at the Henry Phipps Psychiatric Clinic of the Johns Hopkins Hospital, which was built in 1910 in accordance with his plans and which he directed for almost thirty years. Here he perfected the techniques — still widely used — of psychiatric examination and of the accurate recording of case histories.

HILDEGARD WOODWARD, oil on canvas, 19¼ x 16, not dated
Lent by Mrs. Julia L. Asher

EUGENE O'NEILL *Dramatist of the Subconscious* 1888-1953

Eugene O'Neill sought an understanding of man's tragic situation in a universe always mysterious and often hostile. Restlessly experimenting and easily influenced, O'Neill introduced into his plays a variety of dramatic techniques and philosophies that ranged from ancient Greek tragedy and Freudian psychology in *The Great God Brown* (1926) and *Mourning Becomes Electra* (1931) to German expressionism in *The Emperor Jones* (1920) and *The Hairy Ape* (1922). None of them, however, were more than a means to explore his central preoccupation with man's helplessness in the face of forces he cannot understand.

O'Neill was America's first great playwright. His plays were the best offerings of a dedicated band of associates who, influenced by European innovations in theater, transformed American drama from generally superficial entertainment into a serious expression of modern life. This group innovated the "little theater" movement and the off-Broadway production, which gave O'Neill his first audiences.

O'Neill's deeply psychological and haunting plays are not more compelling than his personal drama. His perpetual search for the safety of a "home" was the result of an unstable childhood. The tormented relationship of his unhappy parents and the alcoholism of his beloved brother Jamie are reflected in his last plays — notably in *Long Day's Journey Into Night* (1940) — which at his request were not produced until after his death. He himself lived in increasing isolation, saw his favorite son commit suicide, and died of a crippling nervous disorder.

Zoss Melik, charcoal on paper, 23¼ x 19, not dated
NPG.68.20

Inquirers

America was a provincial outpost of the European scientific tradition at the time of the Revolution. As the frontier rolled back, most Americans were too busy developing the land and acquiring possessions to investigate the world around them; but there have always been a few inquiring spirits eager to "improve the common stock of knowledge," as Benjamin Franklin stated at the founding of the American Philosophical Society in Philadelphia in 1743.

For long the domain of the gifted and enthusiastic amateur, American science was at first concerned with collecting, observing, describing, and classifying the natural wonders of America — a lover's anatomy of the new land. Thomas Jefferson, over a period of many years, collected his Notes on the State of Virginia (1785) because he thought the information about his country being circulated by European naturalists was inaccurate and unworthy.

Although richly endowed with natural resources, the United States for nearly a century was poor in institutions that could foster research and provide suitable careers for the scientific-minded. In the nineteenth century, however, professional scientists — trained in Europe or in newly founded graduate centers — began to replace the amateur practitioners of the eighteenth century. At the same time the field of natural science was broadened when the federal government sponsored exploring expeditions which brought back specimens of rocks, flora, and fauna. American botanists like Asa Gray and John Torrey and the Swiss-American zoologist Louis Agassiz won international reputations, as did a number of American geologists, meteorologists, and paleontologists. Late in the century the American inquirer, with his usual practicality, turned more to agricultural and medical research. He also took up meteorology and, particularly, astronomy, exercising the American inventive bent in the development of astronomical instruments. In 1832 there were no observatories in America; in 1882 there were 144.

DAVID RITTENHOUSE *Watcher of the Skies* **1732-1796**

David Rittenhouse was a clockmaker and instrument-maker by occupation but an astronomer and a mathematician by aptitude and inclination. Without having received a formal education Rittenhouse constructed the first telescope made in America — to observe the transit of Venus in 1769 — and in 1767 he designed his celebrated orrery, an apparatus for illustrating the motions and positions of the planets. Optics, electricity, natural history, and physics were other fields in which he made investigations. Rittenhouse was less interested in the practical application of the facts disclosed by his studies than he was in the pursuit of knowledge for its own sake. He did use his skills, however, to make and repair instruments for George Washington and to conduct boundary surveys and commissions for more than half the colonies.

Rittenhouse became a professor of astronomy at the University of Pennsylvania (1779-1782) and member of its board of trustees as well as a member of the American Philosophical Society and, later, its president (1791-1796) — all without having earned a college degree. A modest retiring man, he was respected by those who knew of his work. Thomas Jefferson wrote of him: "He has not, indeed, made a world, but he has by imitation approached nearer its Maker than any man from Creation to this day."

A patriot as well as a scientist, Rittenhouse was an engineer for the Committee of Safety in 1775, a delegate to the Pennsylvania Constitutional Convention in 1776, and the first director of the United States Mint, from 1792 to 1795.

Charles Willson Peale, who painted this portrait, was a great friend and admirer of the astronomer. They shared the trade of making and repairing clocks; they experimented together, early in the War of Independence, with gunpowder and rifles; and they were leaders in the same left-wing political group.

CHARLES WILLSON PEALE, oil on canvas, 30 x 25, 1772
Lent by University of Pennsylvania, Philadelphia, Pennsylvania

JOHN JAMES AUDUBON *America's Foremost "Birder"* **1785-1851**

John James Audubon — the subject as much of legend as of history — has been hailed as a preserver of wildlife, when he was actually a great hunter. And he has been honored as a pioneer, when much of his life was spent in the eastern United States and Great Britain.

Born in Santo Domingo and raised in France, Audubon spent his middle years traveling throughout America and in England. An out-of-doors naturalist with no formal scientific training or aptitude for scholarship, he was more of an artist and a lover of nature than a scientist. He was no dilettante, however, for only single-purposed industry and determination enabled him to complete his task in the face of poverty and many disappointments.

Audubon made significant contributions to American ornithology, and he set a new standard for the illustration of works on natural history with his life-size drawings of birds "in action." His two greatest works are *The Birds of America* (1827-1838) and *Ornithological Biography* (1831-1839). While some artists have found his bird drawing too photographic and ornithologists have criticized his work for being inaccurate and impressionistic, Audubon still remains for most Americans and Europeans the foremost authority on the birds of this country.

G. P. A. HEALY, oil on canvas, 50¾ x 40½, 1838
Lent by The Museum of Science, Boston, Massachusetts

MATTHEW MAURY   *Scholar of the Sea*   **1806-1873**

Matthew Maury was a professional naval officer who viewed the sea less as the subject of romance and adventure than as that of a distinct branch of science. In 1836 he wrote the first work of nautical science by an American naval officer, and in 1855 he published the first textbook on modern oceanography in English. As superintendent of the United States Navy's Depot of Charts and Instruments (1842-1861) Maury conducted extensive researches on wind and currents. His oceanographic charts for the Atlantic, Pacific, and Indian Oceans shortened the traveling time of ships around the world. And his topographical map of the ocean floor of the North Atlantic illustrated the most practical route for a transoceanic cable. His work led to an international congress in 1853 at Brussels where his system of recording oceanographic data was adopted for all naval and merchant marine ships.

With the outbreak of the Civil War, Maury resigned his United States commission and became a commander in the Confederate Navy. In that role he devised submarine torpedoes and electric mines for use against the Union Navy. From 1862 to 1865 he was in England as an agent of the Confederate Government to procure ships and supplies.

Maury returned to the United States in 1868 to accept a professorship in meteorology at the Virginia Military Institute, where he spent his remaining years. Deeply interested in education and naval reform, Maury's efforts led to the creation of the Naval Academy at Annapolis.

GEORGE W. L. LADD, oil on ivory, 2½ x 2, about 1835
Lent by The Mariners Museum, Newport News, Virginia

LOUIS AGASSIZ *Curious Teacher*   1807-1873

Whether living on the top of a glacier in Switzerland, as he did in 1840, or tramping around the wilds of Brazil, as in 1865, Louis Agassiz was perpetually fulfilling the role of the natural historian in the nineteenth-century sense of the word: He was interested in biology, geology, and anatomy not as separate sciences but as closely related disciplines in the study of the physical world. The Swiss-born scientist traveled throughout Europe, the United States, and Latin America, first to receive training in medicine and biology and then to investigate glacial movements, coastal formations, and the Gulf Stream. As a naturalist he was also interested in the classification of animals and sea life.

Agassiz was not only a distinguished scientist but a great teacher. In 1848 he accepted the chair of natural history at Harvard, a position he held — except for an interval of three years — until his death. Stressing the study of nature by direct observation over textbook learning, he conducted numerous field expeditions and made his influence felt both in the classroom and in the zoological museum that he founded at Harvard. As a regent of the Smithsonian Institution he thought that its real purpose should be research, and that museum collections should be exhibited for the purposes of education and of study. Almost every notable teacher of natural history in the United States in the second half of the nineteenth century was at some time taught by Agassiz or by one of his students.

Although a friend of many of the great men of his time — including Joseph Henry, Ralph Waldo Emerson, Henry Wadsworth Longfellow, Henry David Thoreau, and William James — Louis Agassiz would talk for hours to the man in the street about his scientific work. In a poem dedicated to Agassiz on his fiftieth birthday Longfellow said of him:

He wandered away and away with Nature,
*   The dear old nurse,*
Who sang to him night and day,
*   The rhymes of the universe.*

WALTER INGALLS, oil on canvas, 36¼ x 30¼, not dated
NPG.66.28

ALBERT MICHELSON   *Luminarist*   **1852-1931**

The scientific career of Albert Michelson can be summarized virtually in the word "light." His inquiries into measuring the velocity of light preoccupied him throughout his life and helped to lay the groundwork for Einstein's theory of relativity. By virtue of the accuracy and brilliance of his work, Michelson belongs in a small group of pioneer American physicists that includes Benjamin Franklin, Joseph Henry, and Josiah Willard Gibbs.

Michelson's scientific pursuits were marked by singleness of purpose and clarity of objective. Although he was an instructor in physics and chemistry at his alma mater, the United States Naval Academy, for four years (1875-1879) and head of the department of physics at the University of Chicago for thirty-five (1892-1927), Michelson showed little enthusiasm for the classroom. An unhurried, serene man, he explored the frontiers of physics unruffled by events in the mundane or academic worlds around him.

Moved by curiosity and delight in his research, Michelson was an artist both in his profession and in his recreation. He was a graceful tennis player, a violinist, and an exceptional painter of watercolors; but he felt that only in pure science could art find its highest expression.

RALPH CLARKSON, oil on canvas 50 x 40, 1922
Lent by Harper Memorial Library, University of Chicago, Chicago, Illinois

137

GEORGE WASHINGTON CARVER *Alchemist of Southern Agriculture* **1864-1943**

George Washington Carver was born into slavery in war-torn Missouri, but died an honored scientist whose advice was respected by governments, royalty, and industrial leaders as well as by thousands of ordinary citizens. Overcoming great odds, Carver received his master's degree from Iowa State University in 1896 and soon afterwards accepted Booker T. Washington's offer of a post at Tuskegee Institute in Alabama. He spent nearly forty years at Tuskegee teaching scientific agriculture and conducting research on crop production, nutrition, chemistry, genetics, and plant pathology.

A lifelong interest in breeding beautiful varieties of the amaryllis is represented in the portrait shown here. Carver's main contribution to science, however, was the extraction of new products from previously untapped sources. He developed from the peanut more than three hundred synthetic products, ranging from margarine and flour to marble and axle grease. In the sweet potato he found more than a hundred products, including library paste and rubber. Pecans, okra fiber, soybeans, wild plums, Alabama clay, and cowpeas also yielded to him their useful secrets. His research into the peanut and the sweet potato gave the South alternatives to soil-exhausting cotton as a cash crop. Carver's mobile laboratory spread these and other discoveries throughout the countryside. As a pioneer in synthetics and in dehydration he laid the foundation for important later developments.

A talented artist as well as a concert pianist, Carver chose practical science as his lifework in order to serve more effectively his fellow man, for he felt that "no individual has any right to come into the world and go out of it without leaving behind him distinct and legitimate reasons for having passed through it."

BETSY GRAVES REYNEAU, oil on canvas, 45 x 35, not dated
Gift of the George Washington Carver Memorial Committee **NPG.44.1**

138

The American Is . . .

. . . an Organizer

From the beginning our people have markedly combined practical capacity for affairs with power of devotion to an ideal. The lack of either quality would have rendered the possession of the other of small value.

Theodore Roosevelt,
Speech in Philadelphia, November 22, 1902

If initially the American was forced by the isolation and rigors of frontier life to be resourceful and versatile, he applied these virtues to the highly efficient organization of his means of survival — as restored New England villages, southern plantations, and western settlements testify. Later, the specialization of a highly industrial society and the sheer size of the American's enterprises called upon his organizational skills even further. But behind any enterprise, however modest or ambitious, there is invariably a highly motivated individual with a clear sense of direction, indomitable will, exceptional energy, and managerial skill. With a few notable exceptions, the American from his earliest days has exercised his individuality through an organization; his self-reliance is collective.

As he pushed back the frontier, revealing the boundless expanses and resources of a great continent, the American was impatient to garner for himself a part of this obvious wealth. Having gained control of the land in all its abundance, he has often considered it his God-given duty to make it or its fruits available to others, particularly when large earnings were to be had for the doing. With so much to be done over so vast an area, a premium has been placed upon speed and efficiency, and these, in turn, have required organization. Nowhere has the American's organizational genius been more dramatically demonstrated than in the speed and efficiency with which he built the nation's trade, industry, transportation, and finance.

This capacity for organization, now known around the world, has shown itself in many ways. Some great American organizers have applied their exceptional talents to the accumulation of wealth and the stockpiling of this world's goods. Others, largely indifferent to personal wealth, have concentrated their energies and talents upon service to their fellowman. Although often as single-minded and relentless as robber barons, the humanitarians have been altruistic, while their counterparts have been largely motivated by self-interest and self-aggrandizement. To a certain extent the rugged individualists have produced the altruists — the exploitation of labor by early capitalists making Jane Addams and Samuel Gompers inevitable, just as the Gilded Age and the Roaring Twenties necessitated a period of reform. Nevertheless, among many men of property — Andrew Carnegie, Henry Ford, Andrew Mellon, John D. Rockefeller — the acquisitive instinct was balanced by their later philanthropy. Both impulses, the materialistic and the humanitarian, have long existed in the American character and are far from mutually exclusive. Both derive from the realities under which the country was settled, and both are latent in the Puritan ethos.

Rugged
Individualists

Many elements in the American's growth have contributed to his quest for riches — the Puritan ethic of hard work, thrift, and expectation of tangible rewards for virtue; the enforced frugality of the empty-handed immigrant; the challenge of a new continent with vast untapped resources; and the provincial's respect for possessions as a symbol of hard-won, newly achieved status. On the frontier a man's worth was measured not by his formal education or ancestry but by his capacity to produce the necessities of life for himself and his neighbors. In the developed communities that followed, his worth has been measured by his capacity to produce riches and accumulate possessions. Small wonder that foreigners sometimes feel that our patron deity is not Columbia but Mammon.

The American is said to worship a "success" that is defined as material wealth. If Horatio Alger's heroes were luckier than most young men in real life, they deserved what they got. Most people do, according to the American creed. A chronic labor shortage and hence plenty of jobs from the beginning of our history through much of the present century have been a chief attraction to the immigrant; they have kept alive the belief that no one who is neither ill nor stupid need be poor if he is willing to work. The tycoon who has worked his way to riches is a national folk hero, especially when he has returned much of his great fortune to the people in generous endowments.

The man of wealth is also a popular villain. In a competitive economy, he is often accused of having exploited labor, shortchanged the consumer, or crushed anyone who stood in his way. But even so, the grudging admiration accorded one whose cleverness enables him to get away with a little sharp practice reveals the deep ambivalence in the American attitude toward its capitalists.

SIR WALTER RALEIGH   *Gentleman Entrepreneur*   **about 1554-1618**

The familiar picture of Raleigh, beribboned, bejewelled, and beruffed, while quite accurate in one setting, misrepresents today the man who, at thirty, possessed the organizational ability to plant an English settlement at Roanoke Island. With his half-brother Sir Humphrey Gilbert and the geographer Richard Hakluyt, Raleigh believed that colonies would make England self-sufficient and strong in her struggle with Spain.

Beginning with two ships sent out in 1584 to explore the land, he outfitted and directed five separate expeditions of several ships each during this first Virginia "plantation." For the actual colonizing expeditions of 1585 and 1587, he designed a government and recruited settlers, including women and children. He also chose sea routes and instructed that ships stop in the West Indies to take on horses, agricultural implements, and seeds.

With exceptional resourcefulness and versatility, Raleigh provided for every contingency but one: the failure of his subordinates to carry out his directions. War with Spain prevented him from coming ever to North America, and he saw his great project founder on poor leadership made worse by bad luck. The "lost colony" had demonstrated that "it is a difficult thing to carry over colonies into remote countries upon private men's purses." The next attempt was made by the joint-stock Virginia Company, but Raleigh's novel idea of transplanting whole families to the New World was continued.

Raleigh's son Walter, eight years old at the time of this painting, was killed about fifteen years later by Indians while accompanying his father on an expedition to South America.

UNIDENTIFIED ARTIST, oil on canvas, 78½ x 50⅛, 1602
Lent by National Portrait Gallery, London, England

JOHN JACOB ASTOR *Fur Factor*   **1763-1848**

John Jacob Astor, a German butcher's son, came to America in 1783 for a single purpose: to make money. At that time the Indian fur trade in America was over three hundred years old, but its greatest days were to come. Astor's merchandising instinct flourished in the barter and exchange of the fur trade. No deal was too small or too large for him — he dickered for one skin as he did for a hundred. As the new country expanded, so did Astor's opportunities. By 1800 he had amassed a fortune of $250,000. He pushed farther into the wilderness, then entered trade with China and Europe, and bought up New York City real estate.

To realize his one dream, the monopoly of American fur traffic, Astor organized a chain of fur posts from the Great Lakes to the Pacific, and in 1800 he established Astoria at the mouth of the Columbia River for transshipment of skins to Canton. The War of 1812 ended this enterprise prematurely when the British seized the post, but he recouped the loss by lending money to the United States Government at an exorbitant rate of interest. Astor died the richest man in America, leaving a fortune of more than $20 million.

JOHN WESLEY JARVIS, oil on canvas, 30 x 24¾, not dated
Lent by Mrs. Peter A. Jay

CORNELIUS VANDERBILT   *Transportation King*   **1794-1877**

When Cornelius Vanderbilt was born on a Staten Island farm the United States still clung to the threshold of an unknown continent; when he died the country was covered with a network of railroads, many of which belonged to him. Vanderbilt was no innovator, but he pioneered in the history of American business monopoly. He appropriated new techniques in steamship and rail transportation, which he used with reckless energy and indifference to custom to create an enormously profitable empire. At his death he left one of the great American railway systems and early industrial fortunes — more than $100 million — to the Vanderbilt dynasty he had founded.

The "Commodore," as Vanderbilt came to be called in his steamship days, was a big, handsome, vigorous man. Almost illiterate, he kept his accounts in his head or, according to legend, in an old cigar box. Uneasy with the refinements of polite society, he took on the trappings of wealth only to symbolize his vast power and prove to the world that he was smarter than anybody else.

HIRAM POWERS, marble, 24½ high, 1853
Lent by Vanderbilt University, Nashville, Tennessee

144

MARSHALL FIELD *Merchant Chief* **1834-1906**

Following such pioneers as A. T. Stewart in New York and John Wanamaker in Philadelphia, Marshall Field, a New Englander by birth, brought the Yankee peddler's trade to a high point of retail merchandising. Field made his Chicago department store famous for the quality of its merchandise and for the network he established to stock its shelves. He sent purchasing agents all over the world, bought the entire output of many domestic factories, and had other goods manufactured in his own factories. After he had acquired large supplies he set about creating a demand for what he had to sell. He personally supervised an astonishing number of details and gradually bought out his part-

ners, including Potter Palmer. A man who left nothing to chance, he prepared an elaborate will that entailed Marshall Field and Company and extensive holdings in Chicago real estate to his descendants through the second generation.

Field was criticized for his indifference to everything but business and family, but he contributed to a number of philanthropies in the Chicago area. Perhaps he found his greatest satisfaction, however, in endowing a library for his hometown, Conway, Massachusetts; at its dedication he made the only public speech of his life.

LÉON-JOSEPH FLORENTIN BONNAT, oil on canvas, 49½ x 40, 1903
Lent by Field Enterprises, Inc.

ANDREW CARNEGIE *Evangelist of Wealth* **1835-1919**

According to Andrew Carnegie's "gospel of wealth" set forth in an article he published in 1889, a man should spend the first half of his life acquiring riches and the latter half distributing them. He designed his own career to illustrate this concept of the exceptional man as a steward of public interests.

From weaver's cottage to Skibo Castle in Scotland, from bobbin boy to steel magnate in America — Carnegie's story is a familiar one because he told it so often. Coming to the United States in 1848 with his impoverished Scottish parents, he found his first job in a spinning mill. He educated himself and practiced thrift along with other nineteenth-century virtues until he was able to launch himself in the iron industry

in 1862. Sixteen years later he converted his furnaces to the Bessemer process or, as he explained it, put all his eggs in one basket and watched the basket. In 1900 the Carnegie Company, a limited partnership in which profits were distributed only to working associates, made $40 million; Carnegie's personal share was $25 million. He drove a hard bargain when he sold out in 1901 to the Morgan interests, which formed the billion-dollar United States Steel Corporation.

The doughty Scotsman was as generous as his "gospel" required. Most of his endowments bear his name, and he is more often remembered as a philanthropist than as a hard-driving businessman.

ANDERS ZORN, oil on canvas, 42 x 32, 1911
Lent by Museum of Art, Carnegie Institute, Pittsburgh, Pennsylvania

JAY GOULD   *Machiavelli of Wall Street*   **1836-1892**

Jay Gould, financier and railroad executive, enjoyed power and gardening. The dark little man with the deceptively gentle voice could not be moved by appeals to vanity or sentiment. Exploiting the lack of business ethics in his day, he bribed government officials and manipulated the stock market. His attempt to corner the gold market precipitated the "Black Friday" crash of 1869.

Many Americans admired Gould for the resource-

fulness and daring with which he looted his own enterprises — from the Erie Railroad to Western Union Telegraph. Indifferent to public opinion and the company of friends, he was content in his loneliness. Unlike his flamboyant partner, Jim Fisk, he did not require theater queens, handsome carriages, and flashy vests. He died at fifty-seven in his Gothic castle, near his hothouses full of the flowers that he loved to grow.

Attributed to EASTMAN JOHNSON, oil on canvas, 29½ x 23½, not dated
Lent by National Trust for Historic Preservation, Washington, D. C.

147

MARK HANNA *Big Business Manager*   1837-1904

"God's in his Heaven, all's right with the world!" read Mark Hanna's jubilant telegram to President-Elect McKinley when the vote was counted in 1896. Hanna's powerful and well-financed Republican organization had elected a safely conservative President. Businessmen had feared a revolution of labor anarchists and agrarian radicals under the spellbinding leadership of William Jennings Bryan, but now they could enjoy the prospect of an administration dedicated to their interests.

Hanna's pronouncements were seldom so rhapsodic as his message to McKinley. More characteristic was his observation that in a democracy all questions of government are questions of money. Having acquired a fortune from street railways in Cleveland, Ohio, he applied his business expertise to organizing and financing the Republican Party. By assessing corporations for funds to be spent "where they would do the most good," he raised the record-setting sum — for a single campaign — of $3½ million. Appeals for votes were tailored to please every group of constituents. On election day, "floaters," whose votes were for sale, were marched to the polls with a ballot in one hand and a cash payment in the other. Hanna took no chances when it came to a choice of an election or revolution. His own reward was the chairmanship of the Republican national committee and, in 1897, election to the Senate, where he remained a champion of "stand-pattism" until his death.

ANDERS ZORN, oil on canvas, 45½ x 42, 1908
Lent by The Western Reserve Historical Society, Cleveland, Ohio

JAMES J. HILL   *Colossus of the Northwest*   1838-1916

Empire builder of the Great Northwest, James J. Hill extended his vast railroad system to capture river ports and rail centers, mountain passes and valley routes. In 1878 he purchased a bankrupt railroad, the St. Paul and Pacific, which under his management was so successfully rebuilt and extended that by 1890 it had grown into the Great Northern system. He then allied himself with J. P. Morgan's Northern Pacific Railroad in order to eliminate dangerous and unprofitable competition. A struggle between Hill and E. W. Harriman for control of the Northern Pacific precipitated the panic of 1901. The Northern Securities Company, a holding company which Hill organized in 1901 to consolidate further his transcontinental empire, was attacked under the Sherman Anti-Trust Act and, in 1904, was forced to liquidate by Supreme Court decision.

Alone of all the transcontinental lines, Hill's rail-road network survived financial crises and met every dividend. Using new methods for transporting freight, his lines anticipated future traffic demands, reduced operation costs, and, reversing the practice of other roads, stressed large volume with low rates. Hill personally supervised the construction and administration of his roads, without assistance or interference from the government.

The rail king applied his talents to a variety of other activities, believing it would help business. He was an advocate of trade with the Orient, a leader in the conservation movement, director of several banks, a lecturer on agriculture, and a major backer of Grover Cleveland in the election of 1884. A dynamic, hard-driving, and sometimes violent man, Hill was also an avid reader who took pride in his ability to recite the poems of Burns from memory.

HENRI CARO-DELVAILLE, oil on canvas, 40½ x 36, 1913
Lent by G. Richard Slade

JOHN D. ROCKEFELLER *Benevolent Monopolist*   **1839-1937**

Ten years after John D. Rockefeller had incorporated the Standard Oil Company of Ohio in 1870, this first great modern industrial combine controlled nearly all the refining and transportation of oil in the world. Believing that unlimited competition was inefficient and destructive, Rockefeller brought order to a chaotic industry by buying out rivals willing to sell and crushing those who were not.

"The American beauty rose," he explained to his Baptist Sunday school class, "can be produced . . . only by sacrificing the early buds which grew up around it. This is not an evil tendency in business. It is merely the working-out of a law of nature and a law of God."

A devout churchgoer who scorned personal luxury, Rockefeller dispensed his great private fortune to a public that despised his "tainted money." He eventually overcame this hostility through philanthropies that were as efficiently organized as his business. Of these the broadest in purpose is the Rockefeller Foundation, established in 1913 "to promote the well-being of mankind throughout the world."

PAUL MANSHIP, plaster, 21½ high, not dated
Lent by National Collection of Fine Arts, Smithsonian Institution

THOMAS A. EDISON   *Entrepreneur of Research*   **1847-1931**

The "invention factory" employing more than fifty men that Thomas A. Edison established in 1876 at Menlo Park, New Jersey, was the prototype of the great research laboratories of the twentieth century. Deeply interested in chemistry from an early age, Edison produced a large number of far-ranging inventions, including the phonograph, a commercially practical incandescent lamp, and the rapid-fire shutter which made possible the motion picture camera. But many of the nearly 2,000 patents registered in his name resulted from experiments by groups of laboratory workers working under his direction.

Rough, uncouth, and inclined to spit on the floor and to swear, Edison had acquired somewhat more polish by the time he had organized central electric power

stations into a great utility company and set up a number of factories to manufacture his products. Later, these holdings were consolidated into the General Electric Company. More interested in devices that could be put to commercial use than in commerce itself, he lost interest in his companies and returned to investigation and invention. Although deafness prevented easy intimacy with others, he was, like Andrew Carnegie and John D. Rockefeller, a shrewd judge of men — one who chose gifted assistants and placed them where their contribution would be greatest.

In this portrait by Anderson, Edison is listening to the first message recorded on a wax cylinder and transmitted by phonograph — "Mary Had a Little Lamb."

MRS. POTTER PALMER *Lady Volunteer*   **1849-1918**

Berthe Honoré Palmer had shrewd business sense, managerial talent, and a social conscience. When her husband's real estate interests were destroyed in the Chicago fire of 1871, he rebuilt them with her aid. In 1891 she was chosen chairman of the Board of Lady Managers of the World's Columbian Exposition at Chicago, where she worked tirelessly to ensure women fair representation. Because of her success in this endeavor President McKinley made her a member of the American Committee to the Paris Exposition in 1900.

Mrs. Palmer supported such causes as women's rights and arbitration of labor-management disputes, but she was no crusader in bloomers. Leader of Chicago society, she organized and presided with lovely grace at its annual charity ball, the supreme event of the season. Her gowns by Worth, her jewelry, and the Palmer castle with its red velvet ballroom and famous art gallery reflected the best fashionable taste. With clear consciences the Palmers enjoyed their wealth and social position as a natural reward for their hard work and generosity in building Chicago.

GUERRINO GUARDABASSI, pastel on paper board, 26½ x 20½, about 1893
Lent by Potter Palmer

GEORGE EASTMAN *Kodak King*   **1854-1932**

George Eastman provides a living example of the Horatio Alger success formula. At the age of fourteen, while his widowed mother took in boarders, he left school to take a job as an office boy in a Rochester, New York, insurance office. He had been interested in photography since childhood, but impecuniousness and frugality made him impatient with improving conventional techniques. In 1879 he conceived a better and cheaper photographic process through the commercial use of dry plates. In rapid succession, he then marketed the first Kodak, using paper-backed film; helped to prepare a transparent, flexible film; and began the manufacture of daylight-loading film and the pocket Kodak. By the turn of the century an inexpensive, easily operated camera was within the reach of the man in the street. Gadget-loving Americans soon became avid "shutterbugs" and beat a path to Eastman's factory.

Within the decade 1891-1900, Eastman developed his company into a $10 million business. At one time the Eastman Kodak Company controlled eighty percent of the domestic production of photographic equipment. Impatient and autocratic, Eastman discharged close associates who did not agree with him and suc-

cessfully battled to monopolize the industry. In spite of antitrust litigation brought against his monopoly by President Wilson's administration, he placed the full resources of his company at the disposal of the federal government during World War I; he not only refused war profits but frequently returned government payments.

George Eastman never married. As his immensely profitable business brought him increased wealth, he directed his interest largely to philanthropy. His total benefactions reached to well over $75 million. Perhaps because his father had been an educator (he had founded at Rochester the nation's first business college), Eastman took a special interest in colleges and universities. The University of Rochester, Massachusetts Institute of Technology, and Hampton and Tuskegee Institutes received generous endowments. Most of his largest gifts were made anonymously. It could not be said of the modest Eastman — as Mr. Dooley said of Andrew Carnegie — that every time he gave away a library, he gave himself away in a speech. In 1932, having accumulated and given away an enormous private fortune, Eastman concluded that his work was over and took his own life.

PAUL NADAR, photograph, 6½ x 4½, not dated
Gift of George Eastman House, Rochester, New York NPG.68.11

ANDREW MELLON *Modern Midas*   **1855-1937**

Andrew Mellon made financial history through his vast enterprises in aluminum, oil, and banking and as Secretary of the Treasury. He was quick to recognize the industrial potential of Pittsburgh, where he had been born into a wealthy family. Assuming control of his father's bank, he underwrote "dangerous risks" and took a substantial share in these industries as a return for his financial backing.

The public knew little of this spare, retiring man when he was appointed Secretary of the Treasury by President Harding in 1921. Continuing in this post under Presidents Coolidge and Hoover until 1932, he practiced governmental economy, reduced the national debt, and lowered taxes. Hailed as "the greatest Secretary of the Treasury since Hamilton," Mellon was a champion of conservative Republican principles and large financial interests. Veterans and farmers condemned him, however, for his opposition to the bonus and farm relief, and liberals criticized him highly for continuing business activity while in office. He was an effective director of the nation's economy in a period of rapid growth and prosperity but did not foresee that rapid investment and stock speculation would lead to the Great Depression.

In spite of his wealth, Mellon lived simply. His one passion was his priceless collection of paintings. In 1937 he donated this collection along with money for a National Gallery of Art to the people of the United States.

OSWALD BIRLEY, oil on canvas, 52½ x 41½, 1933
Lent by the National Gallery of Art, Washington, D. C.

HENRY FORD   *Manufacturer for the New Masses*   1863-1947

Henry Ford organized a process. He systematized the production of Model T's so exactly that, as each car passed on a steadily moving belt, the same screw was tightened at exactly the same point by precisely the same twist of the same worker's tool. The assembly line was born, and by 1925 Ford was turning out a new car every ten seconds. Ford's practical dream of making the automobile available to the average American was the initial motive behind the Ford Motor Company. The large fortune that he amassed was only a by-product.

This lean and wiry industrialist, taut as a spring in

one of his "flivvers," was a paradox. Although he voluntarily gave his employees five dollars a day when the average weekly wage was eleven, he fought labor organization in his plant with a private police force. At Greenfield Village he produced a nostalgic replica of a nineteenth-century farm community just as his "tin lizzies" were ending rural isolation forever. Like a number of the great American tycoons who organized monolithic industries, Ford was conscious of promoting the general welfare but reserved to himself the right of determining what was good for the country.

H. WOLLNER, bronze, 16½ high, 1937
Gift of the Henry Ford Trade School Alumni Association NPG.65.3

WILLIAM RANDOLPH HEARST   *Collector*   **1863-1951**

William Randolph Hearst loved animals, children and his mother; but his insatiable thirst for power made him feared by those who worked for him.

Hearst's passion for collecting began with newspapers. In 1887 he took over his father's San Francisco *Examiner*, and by 1925 he had built a powerful newspaper chain and syndicate. By using color extensively, hiring the best writers, and launching interminable crusades, the Hearst papers had a vast influence on American readers. Their "yellow journalism," a combination of saber rattling and yellow ink,

fed the jingoism responsible for the Spanish-American War.

With the profits from his papers, Hearst turned to collecting magazines, art, real estate, motion pictures, trees, animals, and, finally, people. His estate, "San Simeon," near Los Angeles, was nearly as large as Rhode Island. The one thing he desired most he was unable to buy. He was elected to Congress in 1902, but he never received the presidential nomination which he coveted.

ORRIN PECK, oil on canvas, 46 x 41, not dated
Lent by The Hearst Corporation, San Francisco, California

Altruists

From barn-raisings on the frontier to fund-raisings for today's community chest, the American has always found combined efforts and division of labor the best ways of "getting things done." For all his air of improvisation he is systematic and methodical; and for all his resistance to rigid authoritarianism he is an inveterate "organization man." Whether fashioning a highly competitive business or a church, a PTA group or a world government, he devotes an excessive amount of time and attention to tables of organization, committees, and allocations of money and materials. The successful settlement worker, hospital organizer, or trade unionist may be a born business executive who has seen the light. American foundations are modeled on and most often are founded by large business interests. In this country the Good Samaritan and the Philistine merchant are often on the best of terms — they speak the same language.

JOSEPH BRANT *Noble Savage*   **1742-1807**

Joseph Brant, a Mohawk chief and warrior of the Iroquoian Six Nations, was notorious for his merciless ferocity in frontier skirmishes during the American Revolution. He had been treated as a son by Sir William Johnson, British superintendent of Indian affairs in the Mohawk River Valley, educated in a Christian school, and lionized as a cultivated gentleman by London society. When it came to organizing Indians in defense of their lands, however, he reverted to their methods.

During the Revolution Brant and his tribes joined forces with the British in return for a guarantee to preserve Indian territory. With the defeat of the British, Brant turned from savage warrior to diplomatic statesman. Still fearful of American encroachment, he convoked a grand council of Indians at Sandusky, Ohio, in 1783 to unite the Northwest tribes for peaceful negotiation with the white man. The Indian confederacy, under the delusion that the British would come to its aid, decided on war over Brant's opposition. When "Mad Anthony" Wayne defeated the Indians at the Battle of Fallen Timbers in 1794 Brant withdrew with his Mohawks to a Canadian reserve where he governed in peace until his death.

Ezra Ames, oil on canvas, 30½ x 24½, 1806
Lent by New York State Historical Association, Cooperstown, New York

WILLIAM WHITE *Church Reorganizer* **1748-1836**

The Declaration of Independence brought peculiar problems to the Anglican Church in America, which was a part of the Church of England and the established church in eight of the colonies. It seemed impossible to reconcile political liberation from the home country with continued loyalty to the state church. Many Anglican clergymen and laymen in the colonies had been bitterly opposed to the American Revolution, but not William White, assistant minister at Christ Church, Philadelphia. He became rector of the church when his predecessor returned to England and immediately altered the liturgy to make it appropriate for use in the newly independent United States of America.

The Protestant Episcopal Church of America rose from the wreckage of the Anglican Church, decimated by Loyalist emigration and demoralized after the states called for separation of church and state. Its constitution, assigning a new and major role in Episcopal Church government to the laity, was written largely by William White, who also helped in the American revision of the Book of Common Prayer. By 1787, when he was consecrated, in England, as bishop of Pennsylvania, this conciliatory and retiring minister had quietly succeeded in a revolution of his own.

GILBERT STUART, oil on canvas, 36 x 31, 1795
Lent by The Pennsylvania Academy of the Fine Arts, Philadelphia, Pennsylvania

CLARA BARTON   *Lady of Mercy*   **1821-1912**

Clara Barton was better at organizing supplies and transportation than at managing people and money. Tiny but imperious, she could neither delegate authority nor work for a superior, but she was principally responsible for the establishment of the American Red Cross in 1881.

During the Civil War, virtually unaided, she had furnished supplies to the sick and wounded on battlefields and in temporary hospitals, notably the Old Patent Office in Washington, D. C. Later, when she went abroad for a much-needed rest, she performed similar work for the International Red Cross during the Franco-Prussian War. She returned to the United States determined that her country should recognize the Geneva Convention, which had made the Red Cross possible. It was because of her efforts that the United States Senate ratified the Convention in 1882, thereby officially recognizing the American Red Cross.

As president of the American Red Cross until 1904 Clara Barton was in her glory distributing supplies at scenes of disaster, such as the Galveston Flood where she spent six weeks when she was seventy-nine. But her refusal to share responsibility and her poor bookkeeping brought on a Congressional investigation that prompted her resignation in 1904.

J. E. Purdy, photograph, 13 x 10¼, 1904
Lent by the Library of Congress

160

SAMUEL GOMPERS *Patriarch of American Labor*   **1850-1924**

Cigarmaker Sam Gompers believed that higher wages, shorter hours, and better working conditions were the proper objectives of labor unionism. To achieve these objectives he helped organize fellow cigarmakers into a large international organization that could deal directly with employers rather than with legislatures and politicians. The cigarmakers' union became a model for the organizing of other craftsmen. Under Gompers' direction these unions were gradually consolidated under the American Federation of Labor, established in 1886. Except for one year, this great labor leader served as president of the A. F. of L. until his death in 1924.

Having emigrated from England, Gompers was fa-

miliar with the political orientation of British trade unions and with socialist and Marxist theory. Although he borrowed the structure of international Marxism to organize American unions, Gompers was no revolutionary. He sought for labor only a fair share of capitalist profits and a minimum of government interference.

"My legs are so short I never can run away from a fight," he remarked of his five-foot, four-inch frame; but his massive shoulders and broad forehead made him an impressive figure. With age his conservatism and dignity approached pomposity, but he still commanded a universal respect which was gradually transferred to the entire labor movement.

MOSES DYKAAR, marble, 23½ high, 1924
Lent by National Collection of Fine Arts, Smithsonian Institution

JANE ADDAMS   *Pioneer in Social Work*   **1860-1935**

In 1889 Jane Addams with Ellen G. Starr organized Hull House in an old mansion on Chicago's West Side to attack directly the bleakness and barrenness of the Windy City's slums. There she assembled volunteer artists, musicians, teachers, lawyers, and other professionals to live and participate in the stark industrial community. Hull House became a busy center for cultural activities with a pioneer little-theater group, a music school, a gymnasium, a labor museum, and a community kitchen. In addition, Miss Addams worked with labor and reform groups seeking juvenile courts, factory and tenement-house inspection, workmen's

compensation, and an eight-hour workday for women. For her work in peace and relief organizations after World War I she was a corecipient of the Nobel Peace Prize in 1931.

Despite her executive positions, Jane Addams never assumed an air of masculine efficiency nor did she lose her gift of communicating with simple women and children. Occasionally naive, as when she tried to end World War I by personal visits to European chancelleries, she nevertheless made, through her work at Hull House, a major contribution to the development of settlement-house work in this country.

GEORGE DE FOREST BRUSH, oil on canvas, 27¾ x 23⅝, not dated
Lent by Jane Addams' Hull House, University of Illinois at Chicago Circle, Chicago, Illinois

WILLIAM JAMES MAYO   **1861-1939**   **CHARLES HORACE MAYO**   **1865-1939**

THE MAYO BROTHERS   *Hippocratic Team*

William J. and Charles H. Mayo, with their father, were the only resident physicians at St. Mary's Hospital in Rochester, Minnesota, when it opened in 1889. Since the young Mayos were chiefly interested in surgery, they gradually took on partners to handle diagnosis and general medicine. By 1914 the brothers had assembled a staff of twenty-eight and had constructed the first building to house well-equipped laboratories. Each member of the staff was a specialist who was encouraged to follow his own bent through continued study and research. In this fashion the Mayo Clinic evolved.

The Doctors Mayo were also active in medical societies, a new kind of organization which enabled doctors throughout the nation and the world to share observations and findings. As apostles of new methods of antiseptic surgery the Mayos welcomed an agency for keeping the local practitioner informed and for maintaining high professional standards. Each brother was to serve as president of the American Medical Association.

"Dr. Will," a specialist in abdominal surgery, was reticent and unapproachable; "Dr. Charlie," who developed new techniques in thyroid surgery, was talkative and congenial. Together they provided incomparable leadership for their hospital staff of about two hundred doctors. Without setting out to do so, they had organized a private clinic in the old sense of an institution where young doctors learn by observing the examination and treatment of patients by more experienced professionals, and in the newer sense of a center where a patient benefits from the services of numerous specialists.

Both portraits: LOUIS BETTS, oil on canvas, 71 x 58, about 1922
Lent by Mayo Foundation, Rochester, Minnesota

CHARLES RICHARD DREW   *Lifesaver to Mankind*   **1904-1950**

During the German bombings in 1941 England was in desperate need of blood supplies to care for the thousands of wounded civilians. She turned to America — and particularly to Charles Drew, a brilliant young Negro doctor who was an authority on blood preservation and the operation of blood banks. Drew was appointed director of the Blood for Britain Campaign, with headquarters at Presbyterian Hospital in New York.

Although blood banks already existed, their supplies were inadequate. Often the plasma they received had become contaminated in shipping. With his outstanding organizational ability and extensive knowledge, Dr. Drew solved these problems; within a few months

Britain was receiving the blood supplies she needed. His work was the basis of the American Red Cross blood donor project, of which he was appointed director.

Born in a Washington, D. C., slum, Charles Drew was not unfamiliar with racial discrimination. When the Red Cross announced in 1941 that it would not accept the blood of non-Caucasian donors, Drew resigned quietly and without bitterness. He returned to Howard University where he resumed his mission of training young Negro doctors and where he practiced surgery. When he died in 1950, in an automobile accident, he had trained more than half of the certified Negro doctors in the country.

BETSY GRAVES REYNEAU, oil on canvas, 40 x 30¼, not dated
NPG.67.35

The American...

Blessed assurance,
Jesus is mine!
O, what a foretaste of glory divine!
Heir of salvation, purchase of God,
Born of his spirit, washed in his blood.
This is my story, this is my song
Praising my Savior, all the day long.

Fanny J. Crosby

...Finds God in Divers Ways

The American confidently believes that individuals can be redeemed in this life and that the kingdom of God can be realized in America and, by extension, elsewhere. The pursuit of effective means to these ends explains in large part the diversity and inventiveness of religious faith in this country. At the same time, freedom to move about within the vast reaches of the Atlantic seaboard precluded from the outset political enforcement of religious uniformity except in a few restricted areas. By the time of the American Revolution religious toleration was already the only acceptable or practical arrangement, and was so recognized by the Constitution. Given this combination of faith in man's capacity to work God's will and freedom to experiment, American churches have splintered into deeply committed, self-energizing sects, each enjoying a righteous conviction that it has the key to personal salvation and the abundant life. The typical revival meeting culminating in mass conversions dramatizes, only more sensationally and spontaneously, the entry which all faiths promise into the community of saints on earth.

Yet nearly all American religion, however experimental or exotic, is rooted in historic western Catholicism, the Reformed tradition of Europe, or the ancient faith of the Jews — which have their own common roots. Only recently have increasing numbers in all faiths recognized their essential unity by sharing in a new ecumenical movement and drive for social justice.

INCREASE MATHER   *Puritan Oligarch*   1639-1723

Increase Mather, of the distinguished family of early Congregational clergymen, believed in a stern, righteous God who saved a few elect and damned the rest of mankind to eternal torment. This Calvinist deity, incomprehensible and repellent to most twentieth-century Americans, was for him a beautiful, compelling vision. He described his religious awakening in his *Autobiography:*

. . . in the latter end of May, 1655, I was in extremity of anguish and horror in my soul. . . . I prayed to God that he would show me mercy. . . . as I was praying, I gave myself up to Jesus Christ, and his forever; and humbly professed to him that if I did perish, I would perish at his feet. Upon this I had ease and inward peace in my perplexed soul immediately; and from that day I walked comfortably

for a considerable time, and was careful that all my words and ways should be such as would not offend God.

Mather, however, was not a religious recluse or zealot. Understanding human nature and conciliatory, he was a popular minister of the Second Church of Boston, acting president and rector of Harvard College, a leading figure in Massachusetts politics, and the Colony's agent to England from 1690 to 1692. As interested in science as in theology, he was a strong advocate of smallpox vaccinations in the Colony. His many writings often demonstrated more clarity, vigor of mind, and substance than those of his son Cotton Mather and his fellow Puritans. When he died, he was so influential that a former enemy wrote, "He was the patriarch and prophet among us, if any might be so called."

JAN VAN DER SPRIETT, oil on canvas, 48½ x 40, 1688
Lent by Massachusetts Historical Society, Boston, Massachusetts

JONATHAN EDWARDS *Great Awakener* 1703-1758

When Jonathan Edwards preached on hell, a popular story went, he made it real enough to be found in the atlas. Much more than a preacher of damnation he was also a sensitive pastor, devoted husband and father, a mystic seer, and thinker profound enough to be called "one of the great original minds of America."

Edwards entered Yale just before his thirteenth birthday, having already penned a perceptive essay on spiders. By the time he graduated in 1720 he had filled a notebook with philosophical observations, reconciling Newton's natural law and a divinely ordained universe. For twenty-three years he served as pastor in Northampton, Massachusetts. Edwards became one of the leaders of the "Great Awakening," the evangelical revival stressing personal conversion and supernatural illumination that swept the American Colonies near the middle of the eighteenth century. Anxious that members of his congregation experience "heart religion" as deeply as he had, he examined his converts with care and disallowed responses he considered spurious. But after he began to insist that "visible sainthood" — personal faith supported by a consistent Christian life — was requisite to full communion in the church, his people in 1750 dismissed him.

Concealing his disappointment, Edwards moved his large family to Stockbridge, Massachusetts, a frontier outpost where he preached to the Housatonic Indians, catechised their children, and wrote the books on which his fame as a theologian largely rests. He was summoned from exile to become president of Princeton in 1758, but he died of smallpox a month after assuming the new post.

JOSEPH BADGER, oil on canvas, 30½ x 25½, not dated
Lent by Yale University Art Gallery, New Haven, Connecticut, Bequest of Eugene Phelps Edwards

JOHN CARROLL *Pilot of New Catholicism*   **1735-1815**

A Jesuit when the Society of Jesus was in universal disrepute, devotee of authoritarian religion when his country was declaring independence, American patriot when his best friends were English Loyalists, John Carroll earned his ecclesiastical preeminence by sheer force of character and ability. The Roman Catholic Church made him its first American bishop in 1790 before his coreligionists thought it wise or necessary even to have a bishop. His monument is the entire subsequent development of Roman Catholicism in the United States.

Scion of an old Maryland family, Carroll regarded American freedom as an unparalleled opportunity for the Church. Rome accepted his suggestion that the American clergy be permitted to choose its own bishop, subject only to confirmation by the Holy See. He

founded Georgetown University to train native priests and fostered several other institutions. In 1808 after his "national" diocese had been divided into four, he was elevated to the archbishopric.

Never satisfied with his accomplishments, Carroll's last years were clouded by a sense of failure. His honest administration had not entirely satisfied factions jostling one another in the immigrant Church, and his charity toward some of the Church's troublemakers went unrewarded. A puritanical reserve prevented him from expressing feelings of affection and sympathy; his only close friend was an English correspondent whom he had last seen in 1790. Nevertheless, as chief pilot of his church in the new nation John Carroll faithfully set its course.

GILBERT STUART, oil on canvas, 29 x 24, not dated
Lent by Georgetown University, Washington, D. C.

WILLIAM ELLERY CHANNING   *Evangelical Reformist*   **1780-1842**

The spiritual father of Unitarianism in America was a deeply religious man who regarded reason as the servant, never the enemy, of piety. A child of the Revolutionary era, William Ellery Channing grew up with the new nation and fully shared the optimism of its rationalistic founders. Although he never discarded the devotion of his Puritan forebears, he liberated their harsh Calvinism from its assumptions of human depravity and divine election. His testimony of evangelical conversion nevertheless reads like that of John Wesley and of Jonathan Edwards.

Channing was born in Newport, where as a boy he watched the Rhode Island legislature ratify the Constitution; was educated at Harvard; and in 1803 was installed as minister of the Federal Street Congregational Church, Boston, in which he served until his retirement. Although he believed in God as personal Father and was profoundly reverent toward Jesus Christ, he brooked no orthodoxy — not even a Unitarian one. He preferred "the community of free minds,

of lovers of truth, and followers of Christ, both on earth and in heaven. . . . I can endure no sectarian bonds."

But Channing was a liberal, not a radical. His fragile health did not prevent him from laboring indefatigably to promote practical Christianity. Stressing the dignity of man as revealed in the Christian revelation, he urged the abolition of slavery, war, intemperance, poverty, and prison abuses. And well in advance of his time he advocated public education, labor reform, and an enlightened program to combat intemperance. Critics have detected hints of paternalism in his philanthropy, possibly the lingering vestige of his aristocratic heritage. Nevertheless, as a pilgrim of faith he pushed ahead, seeking a future where men could fulfill their humanity according to the ideal manifested in Jesus Christ. His statue in the Boston Public Gardens bears the inscription, "He breathed into theology a humane spirit."

WASHINGTON ALLSTON, oil on canvas, 31 x 27½, about 1810
Lent by Museum of Fine Arts, Boston, Gift of William Francis Channing

JOSEPH SMITH *Frontier Prophet*

1805-1844

Like other New Englanders transplanted to western New York — a region given to popular superstition and millennial religious sects, Joseph Smith as a boy hunted buried treasure, joined his family (he was one of ten children) in camp meeting revivals, and puzzled over the conflicting claims of rival religions. Looking back nearly two decades to his religious conversion, he once recorded, "So great were the confusion and strife among the different denominations, that it was impossible for a person as young as I was, and so unacquainted with men and things, to come to any certain conclusion who was right and who was wrong." Joseph Smith therefore did what several Americans in similar circumstances have done: He started a new church.

A series of visions in the 1820s revealed to him his divine appointment to restore Christ's church, which Smith and five other men organized in the presence of about thirty converts on 6 April 1830 as the "Church of Christ" (eight years later named "Church of Jesus Christ of Latter Day Saints") at Fayette, New York. In 1830 he published *The Book of Mormon*, an account of ancient Hebrew peoples transplanted to America. Smith claimed to have "translated" miraculously this record from golden plates unearthed three years earlier by angelic direction. Smith was acknowledged as "a prophet, [and] an apostle of Jesus Christ"; the church was admonished to "give heed unto all his words and commandments."

A pilgrimage to establish the City of Zion took the Latter Day Saints to Ohio, to Missouri, and finally to Illinois, where they built Nauvoo into the state's largest city. There Smith exercised arbitrary ecclesiastical and political authority as prophet, mayor, and commanding general of the Nauvoo Legion. In 1844 he announced his candidacy for the United States Presidency.

But Smith's "revelations" regarding celestial marriage (foreshadowing polygamy) and his destruction of an antagonistic press excited the fury of local citizens who jailed him at Carthage, Illinois. On 27 June 1844 he and his brother were shot to death in their cell. Two years later many of Smith's followers began their trek to the Great Salt Lake Valley, in present Utah, while numerous others remained in Illinois and neighboring states.

Unknown artist, oil on canvas, 28¾ x 22¾, not dated
Lent by the Reorganized Church of Jesus Christ of Latter Day Saints, Independence, Missouri

ISAAC MAYER WISE   *American Israelite*   **1819-1900**

By adapting the faith of his fathers to a new social environment, Rabbi Isaac M. Wise earned his title as the "father of American Reform Judaism." In 1846 he came to Albany, New York, from his native Bohemia where state restrictions had prevented efforts to liberalize the Jewish community. He quickly discovered what an energetic pragmatist might accomplish in a land of religious liberty. Throwing himself with great energy into the job of learning English, he was, by the early 1850s, one of only a few rabbis who had full command of the language.

In the tradition of American reform, Rabbi Wise soon split his congregation and led its progressive element to form a new synagogue with updated ritual. In Cincinnati, his base of operations from 1854 to the end of his life, he founded a weekly English newspaper, the *Israelite*, which became *The American Israelite*, and published a modern prayer book. He was the author of many other works, chiefly on Judaic history and theology.

An exceptional organizer rather than a theorist, however, he promoted the cause of liberal Judaism by establishing the Union of American Hebrew Congregations (1873), the Hebrew Union College (1875), and the Central Conference of American Rabbis (1889). He served as president of all three organizations until his death. These institutions, Wise had declared confidently, stood for "the American Israel of the liberal and progressive school." They form a triple memorial to Wise's life work — the welding of ancient Judaic faith with the American spirit.

MOSES JACOB EZEKIEL, marble, 27 high, 1903
Lent by Hebrew Union College, Cincinnati, Ohio

MARY BAKER EDDY   *Spiritual Healer*   **1821-1910**

Saint or devil, healer or charlatan, oracle or plagiarist — Mary Baker Eddy was one of the most controversial figures in American religion. She possessed an uncanny ability to inspire fanatical devotion or bitter antagonism.

Mrs. Eddy at forty-one was a chronic invalid, subject since childhood to hysterical seizures. In 1862, however, after consulting Phineas P. Quimby, who claimed to heal through "spiritual science," she improved so remarkably that she became an apostle of his gospel of mental healing. After years of ill health, destitution, and family misfortunes, she painstakingly evolved her own system of healing which in 1875 she set forth in *Science and Health.* Royalties from subsequent editions of the book eventually made her wealthy.

From small beginnings in Lynn, Massachusetts, the Church of Christ, Scientist, moved to Boston where it was established as the "Mother Church" of a rapidly growing movement.

In later life Mrs. Eddy lived in seclusion, becoming a legend in her own lifetime. The *Journal of Christian Science* claimed that she was "God-sent to the world as much as any character of Sacred Writ," and the devotion of her followers amounted almost to worship. The fact that her quick temper and inflexible will alienated others may simply mean that she was interested more in her message than in people. But the long shadow of that message is a prodigious accomplishment for a frail woman who was penniless and friendless until, at fifty-four, she wrote a little book that offered a new key to life.

LUELLA VARNEY SERRAO, marble, 19 high, including base, about 1888
Gift of Mrs. Frances Thompson Hill and Calvin C. Hill   *NPG.62.11*

DWIGHT L. MOODY   *Revivalism's Supersalesman*   1837-1899

Dwight L. Moody's energy and drive belied his two-hundred-pound hulk and earned him the title of "the lightning Christian." Dissatisfied with life on his family's Massachusetts farm and with clerking in Boston, he went to Chicago at the age of twenty. Moody and Chicago, both young and hustling, were made for each other. He expanded his business activities so shrewdly that he might have amassed one of the great fortunes of the Gilded Age. As it was, he turned his Yankee genius to a full-time religious vocation in 1861 and commandeered the resources of millionaire friends for his evangelistic enterprises.

Moody was always in hot pursuit of souls. He passed easily and naturally from sidewalk soul-winning to Sunday school teaching to lay preaching to professional revivalism. With the organized efficiency of big business and the simplified message of a personable popularizer he persuaded thousands to reaffirm the old-time religion. Teamed with Ira D. Sankey — whose gospel ballads could arrest a hurrying throng or melt a tabernacle audience — Moody assured America's new urban middle class of God's unfailing love and urged them to "take — t-a-k-e, TAKE" the salvation that He graciously offered. He was so persuasive that many of his converts must have thought that God himself looked something like Dwight L. Moody.

Carlo Pellegrini ("Ape"), watercolor on paper, 11¾ x 7⅛, 1875
***Gift of the Trustees of the National Portrait Gallery, London*   NPG.64.7**

The
American
Is . . .

. . . Larger
than Life

Come to Van Horn to live
The climate is so healthy
We had to shoot a man
To start our graveyard

Advertisement quoted by Mody C. Boatright,
Folk Laughter on the American Frontier

In a country of almost incalculable distances and incredible opportunities, the American stands tall, tells tall tales, and builds tall buildings — which he calls "skyscrapers" to make them sound taller. Pride in native endowments and a mock-heroic defense against their terrible immensity have made him a hyperbolist. Exaggeration is deeply engrained in the national character: America's court fools pose as village wags; leading crusaders echo the biblical rhetoric of country preachers. The American is so accomplished in the art of bragging that he boasts as easily in the negative as in the affirmative. What follows appeared in a nineteenth-century American newspaper:

This is a glorious country. It has longer rivers and more of them, and they are muddier and deeper and run faster and rise higher, and make more noise, and fall lower, and do more damage, than the rivers of any other country.

It has more lakes, and they are bigger and deeper, and clearer and wetter, than those of any other country. Our rail-cars are bigger, and run faster, and pitch off the track oftener, and kill more people, than all other rail-cars in this and every other country. Our steamboats carry bigger loads, are longer and broader, bust their boiler oftener, and send up their passengers higher, and the captains swear harder than the steamboat captains in any other country. Our men are bigger and longer and thicker, can fight harder and faster, drink more mean whisky, chew more bad tobacco and spit more and spit farther, than in any other country. Our ladies are richer, prettier, dress finer, spend more money, break more hearts, wear bigger hoops, shorter dresses, and kick up the devil generally to a greater extent than all other ladies in all other countries. Our children squall louder, grow faster, get too expansive for their pantaloons, and become twenty years old sooner by some months, than any other children of any other country on the earth.

Quoted by S. S. Cox
Why We Laugh, 1876

WILLIAM LLOYD GARRISON *Universal Reformer*   **1805-1879**

"I am in earnest — I will not equivocate — I will not excuse — I will not retreat a single inch — and *I will be heard!*" proclaimed William Lloyd Garrison in 1831, in the first issue of *Liberator*, his abolitionist newspaper. Not until the passage of the 13th Amendment abolished slavery thirty-five years later did the *Liberator* cease publication. One of the earliest abolitionists to demand complete and immediate freedom for the Negro, Garrison was irreconcilable to any other settlement of the slavery issue. He scorned the idea of political action and publicly burned a copy of the United States Constitution as a "covenant with death and an agreement with hell" for protecting slavery; instead, he relied on the power of moral principles.

Slavery was not the only evil that Garrison fought. He attacked with equal vigor intemperance, gambling, capital punishment, imprisonment for debt, and a host of other abuses. And abolition was not the only cause he espoused, for he championed pacifism, women's rights, free trade, and justice for the Indians and the Chinese.

A self-righteous, serious man, Garrison sought nothing less than the "redemption of the human race," and he did so with determination and courage. Although at times he was inconsistent and contradictory, Garrison never doubted for a moment the truth and importance of what he preached; for him there was no middle ground between good and evil.

NATHANIEL JOCELYN, oil on panel, 30 x 25, 1833
Lent by Mr. and Mrs. Garrison Norton

PHINEAS T. BARNUM *Marvel-Maker*   1810-1891

For half a century Phineas T. Barnum was the un-rivaled master of ballyhoo and hoax, the great exhibitor who was his own best exhibit. He might well have billed himself "Greatest Showman on Earth."

From obscure origins in Connecticut, Barnum at twenty-five moved into the limelight in New York by touting a lady who purported to be 161 years old and George Washington's nurse. In 1842 he opened his American Museum. There, until it burned to the ground in 1868, Barnum delighted visitors with a much-publicized repertory of freaks, fakes, fantasy, and effrontery — fat women and deformed men, the bearded Madame Clofullia who proved her female sex

in court, the Siamese twins Chang and Eng, a man-made mermaid, the door to the "Egress" which deposited patrons in the alley. Barnum's discovery of "General Tom Thumb," a twenty-five-inch midget, brought him international renown, while his management of Jenny Lind's popular and profitable American tour forced his acceptance as a serious impresario.

In 1871, following a short retirement, Barnum entered the circus world where his flair for advertising again proved successful. His "Greatest Show on Earth" merged with the circus of James A. Bailey in 1881 and, after Barnum's death, with that of the Ringling Brothers.

THOMAS BALL, marble, 30 high, not dated
Lent by Tufts University, Medford, Massachusetts

HARRIET BEECHER STOWE *Righteous Penwoman* **1811-1896**

According to Harriet Beecher Stowe, Abraham Lincoln paid tribute to her antislavery novel, *Uncle Tom's Cabin* or *Life Among the Lowly* (1852), by greeting her as "the little woman who made the book that made the great war." But Mrs. Stowe, the first American author to take the Negro seriously and the first to write a novel with a black man as hero, had written an abolitionist manifesto unwittingly. Her inverted epic of the slave Uncle Tom and his three masters aroused violent sectional passions beyond her greatest expectations and made her famous overnight. Within a year of publication the book's sales reached 300,000.

With the coming of the Civil War, Mrs. Stowe felt that she had been divinely appointed to lead the struggle. She rushed to Washington where she offered

Lincoln her advice and insisted that military officers and cabinet officials keep her informed. She also demanded special privileges for her enlisted son.

One of the most celebrated American women wherever *Uncle Tom's Cabin* was published, Mrs. Stowe found many other causes to champion, including that of Lord Byron's wife, whose sad plight at the hands of a philandering husband she related in *The True Story of Lady Byron's Life* (1869). The daughter, sister, and wife of Calvinist clergymen, Mrs. Stowe struggled with a righteous God throughout her life. The conflict between faith and doubt haunted her until ten years before her death, when she abdicated all responsibilities and drifted into a dreamlike trance in a premature embrace of death.

ALANSON FISHER, oil on canvas, 34 x 27, 1853
NPG.68.1

MARK TWAIN   *Black Humorist*   **1835-1910**

Ernest Hemingway once remarked that "all modern American literature" comes from *The Adventures of Huckleberry Finn* (1884). If that is a native over-statement, it is nevertheless true that Mark Twain (Samuel L. Clemens) was the first American to discover high and poetic art in the colloquial. Twain mined the frontier lode of American humor — exaggeration, the hoax, and deadpan, malapropic wit. And like many other major American writers — from James Fenimore Cooper to Norman Mailer — he was nourished by the exuberant character of the Territory Ahead.

The Adventures of Huckleberry Finn is one of the world's greatest comic novels because it veers so near the tragic. It is, after all, about a boy whose imagination is ridden with visions of disaster and death, who seriously chooses Hell to save his best friend and whose ultimate fate may well be that of his drunken, outcast father. But of course we never learn that fate because Twain, with his prescient sense of the popular, ended the book as Huck seceded from civilization. *The Adventures* recalled Twain's own boyhood days on the Mississippi and the golden days of America "befo' de wo." Afterward, as his country slumped into the Gilded Age, Twain's own humor became blacker. "If you pick up a starving dog and make him prosperous, he will not bite you. This is the principal difference between a dog and a man." And in his later works, like *The Mysterious Stranger* (published posthumously, 1916), he became bleakly determinist in his excoriation of "the damned human race." To the end he inveighed against injustice as he saw it — against American and Western racism, Belgian colonialist brutality in the Congo, and American colonialism in the Philippines.

CHARLES N. FLAGG, oil on canvas, 40¼ x 32⅜, 1890
Lent by The Metropolitan Museum of Art, New York, New York, Gift of Miss Ellen Earle Flagg, 1917

THOMAS NAST *Giant Killer*   **1840-1902**

Since the time of William Hogarth, the eighteenth-century English satirist, the caricature — exaggerating its victims and their foibles — has been an effective means of social and political criticism. Few practitioners of the art have been as successful and influential as Thomas Nast. Building upon well-established English tradition and scattered American predecessors, he virtually created the topical or political cartoon as a weapon of American journalism.

German by birth, Nast was brought to the United States as a child. At fifteen he began doing illustrations for newspapers, and in 1862 became a staff artist for *Harper's Weekly*. From depicting scenes he moved quickly to pictorial editorializing, turning his wrath successively upon Copperheads, "King" Andrew Johnson, the Ku Klux Klan, Horace Greeley, and "dumb" Irishmen.

Nast originated the Republican elephant and popularized the donkey as the Democratic Party symbol. His greatest achievement, however, was his campaign against the corrupt New York political machine, Tammany Hall, and its leader "Boss" Tweed. His grotesque but effective caricatures of Tweed—as a grim, balloon-like, criminal-looking figure — were instrumental in destroying the Tammany machine and sending its leader to jail. "My constituents can't read," complained Tweed, "but damn it, they can see pictures!"

JOHN W. ALEXANDER, oil on canvas, 40 x 30¼, 1887
NPG.66.40

WILLIAM JENNINGS BRYAN *Soldier of the Cross* 1860-1925

"Clad in the armor of a righteous cause," William Jennings Bryan stood before the Democratic National Convention of 1896 and thundered to the crowd: "You shall not press down upon the brow of labor this crown of thorns; you shall not crucify mankind upon a cross of gold." Bryan's emotional rhetoric, with its biblical overtones and righteous ring, swept the ranks of the silver men, who wanted the nation to go off the gold standard, and won for the orator — who was only thirty-six — the presidential nomination of the Democratic Party. The political evangelist and crusader crossed the nation, fighting the "battle of the standards" and preaching the cause of the common people. Throughout the campaign he exhibited the fervor and flaming oratory that was to characterize all of his crusades — for political and economic reform, peace, anti-imperialism, and religious fundamentalism.

As the Democratic candidate in three presidential campaigns (1896, 1900, and 1908) and as Wilson's Secretary of State (1913-1915), Bryan maintained unswervingly his sense of Protestant Christian morality, his faith in the basic goodness of his fellowman, and his belief in the divine destiny of the United States — and of William Jennings Bryan. "When God tells a man to speak," he said, "he cannot stop to count those who stand behind him. He must speak even though he cries in the wilderness; he must stand up even if he has to stand alone."

The "Great Commoner" knew and loved the people of the agrarian West, for he was one of them and spoke to them in their own language. But in his attempt to create a heaven on earth he could not reach the rising numbers of industrial workers in the big eastern cities.

JOSEPH KEPPLER, "The Professional Bridegroom,"
pencil and ink cartoon, published in *Puck*, 29 May 1907, 14¼ x 20¼
Lent by the Library of Congress

181

WILL ROGERS   *Cowboy Philosopher*   **1879-1935**

In 1916 Will Rogers quipped that Woodrow Wilson was "five notes behind" in our negotiations with Germany. Wilson laughed with the rest of the country, for Rogers had again "crystallized" the truth of a situation and had made it seem funny. Making current events his target, Will Rogers joked at whatever party, idea, or fad was most fashionable at the time, while sparing the underdog. "Every time Congress makes a joke, it's a law. And every time they make a law, it's a joke." Through the media of the radio and sound movies Rogers established a new style in popular entertainment — its ingredients a folksy, easy manner, a blend of sentimentality and satire, and an apparently improvisational delivery.

Born in Oklahoma when it was still Indian territory, Will Rogers was of Cherokee extraction on both sides of his family. He was proud of his heritage: "My ancestors didn't come over on the Mayflower; they met the boat." After starting as a cowboy in Texas, he became in 1902 a rope artist and a rough rider in a Wild West circus. He was in turn an actor, a star performer in several productions of the *Ziegfeld Follies*, a special writer for *The New York Times*, a lecturer, a radio speaker, a movie star — and always a humorist and showman.

The strict purity of his language and of his private life contrasted sharply with the jazz age in which he flourished. His personal qualities of decency and generosity had as much to do with his popularity as his ability as an entertainer. An honest, trustful, humble person, with the courage to make dry humor out of America's follies, Will Rogers had a zest for life and a restlessness that was peculiarly American. Close to the grass roots, he always "played his natchell self."

Jo Davidson, bronze, 27 high, 1938
NPG.67.52

The American...

...Seeks an Identity

Society in America was always trying, almost as blindly as an earthworm, to realize and understand itself; to catch up with its own head, and to twist about in search of its tail.

Henry Adams,
The Education of Henry Adams (1918)

Preoccupation with image permeates American life. For example, Americans are the greatest users of cosmetics in the history of the world. They want to save face: the well-to-do patronize face-lifting, nose-straightening, tooth-capping; the less affluent content themselves with fake eyelashes, hairpieces, hairdye, hair curlers, hair straighteners, and hair removers. In a closely contested presidential election, Richard Nixon's defeat in 1960 was widely attributed to the failure of his TV makeup.

Like political leaders, Broadway and Hollywood stars depend on their images for a livelihood and therefore almost never accept bit parts. In the United States it is tacitly assumed, as it is not assumed elsewhere, that only bit players play lesser roles. But the ordinary American citizen is as concerned with his image as national personalities with theirs — with what he is and where he belongs. And what preoccupies individual citizens also preoccupies the corporations, who spend commensurately vaster sums in the maintenance or refurbishing of their images. In preparing "a face to meet the faces that you meet," singularity is often lost in uniformity, the member in the species.

At a more serious level, the problem of image becomes the crisis of identity. "What is Jack Paar *really* like?" Or, as American art historians obsessively ask, "What is American about American art?" Or, as the question the present exhibition poses, "What is an American?" If there is anxiety about the answer, it is because Americans fear that if they cannot define who they are they will have to admit they really do not exist — that they are nothing more than a collection of refugees. The American feels he must find a name for himself in order to assert his reality. In this version of the existential predicament, Americans would like to reverse Descartes' reasoning to say: "We are; therefore we think — and know how to act as a nation."

The American dilemma, intricately difficult for the white man, is even harder for the Negro, for he has still not risen completely from the nonbeing of slavery. Locked in a painful struggle with the past, most Americans prefer the Party of Hope to the Party of Memory: face-saving, and for those buildings they do not demolish, re-facing. They would destroy their heritage as they destroy those leaders who confront them with the burden of their past, so inseparably linked to the burden of their future — their own "selves."

Interpreters
and
Imagemakers

Artists make experience real, as translators make language understandable. They mythicize experience and interpret us to ourselves; they therefore are not just artists but unacknowledged legislators. In his Letters from an American Farmer *(1782), Jean de Crèvecoeur asked the question preliminary to art around which this exhibition is predicated: "What then is the American?" The answer is a paradoxical one: A stereotype to other men, the American is all things to himself. America's first distinguished respondent was Benjamin Franklin who in his* Autobiography *displays such enduringly American characteristics as unembellished style, native wit and shrewdness, resilient optimism, boundless versatility, a pragmatic manner, and the notion that hard work will necessarily turn rags into riches. Franklin's dialectical opposite, Jonathan Edwards, the Calvinist theologian of "Sinners in the Hands of an Angry God," assures us of God's vindictiveness, man's overwhelming insufficiency, and the proximity of his eternal damnation — as proximate as that of a spider dangling over a flaming pit.*

In the nineteenth century Emerson and Whitman pronounce the infinitude of the private self; Hawthorne and Melville, its necessary limitation. Cooper dramatizes the rigid code of the frontier; James, the subtleties of the drawingroom. Winslow Homer paints the American landscape and seascape with fidelity and particularization; Albert Pinkham Ryder, with a light ne'er seen on land or sea. Thomas Eakins presents his sitters in contemplation of their inner selves; John Singer Sargent, with a bravura handling of their outer charms.

From the outset, in other words, the interpretation of the American experience has proceeded dialectically; and in a significant manner in the work of many of the country's best modern artists it still proceeds so: William Faulkner and Ernest Hemingway, T. S. Eliot and William Carlos Williams, Frank Lloyd Wright and Philip Johnson, Martha Graham and George Balanchine, David Smith and Alexander Calder, Jackson Pollock and Stuart Davis. These pairs of artists may be said to reveal alternate visions of America and Americans — opposing but far from mutually exclusive interpretations.

CHARLES BULFINCH   *Palladio of the New Republic*   1763-1844

Charles Bulfinch was renowned in his time for his public service. Called the "Great Selectman" by his contemporaries, he served on Boston's board of selectmen for twenty-five years and was chairman for eighteen. He also served his community and his nation as an architect, and perhaps it is true that of all artists the architect has the best opportunity for creating public works of both usefulness and beauty. While he was an official and city architect, old Boston developed from a sprawling, overgrown village around a neglected common into a handsome capital city with parks, crescents, and distinguished municipal buildings.

Architectually self-taught, Bulfinch followed a European tour suggested to him by Thomas Jefferson and returned to America with memories of neoclassical motifs which he subtly adapted and imaginatively refined to meet American requirements. Most famous in New England for his Massachusetts State House and Faneuil Hall — the State House became a prototype

for other official structures — Bulfinch also built Boston's first theater and elsewhere in New England a prison, a hospital, school buildings, and more than forty churches. In domestic architecture he introduced the style of the Adam brothers into New England, and for the first time in America conceived a row of town-houses in a unitary design.

In 1817 at the behest of President Monroe, Bulfinch took charge of the project to complete the National Capitol and saw it through to its completion in 1830; his own distinctive and particular contribution was the detailed articulation of the west facade.

Bulfinch's achievement as an artist was the infusion of traditional European forms with a new simplicity, dignity, and repose befitting the young nation's image of itself. Like John Singleton Copley, he distilled an esthetic purity from a Puritan heritage, and, as that latter-day Puritan Henry David Thoreau once recommended, got the palaver out of his style.

MATHER BROWN, oil on canvas, 30 x 25¼, 1786
Lent by Fogg Art Museum, Cambridge, Massachusetts

JAMES FENIMORE COOPER   *American Dreamer*   **1789-1851**

James Fenimore Cooper is our first novelist to produce a significant body of fiction. Not a prose master — if anything he was master of the ill-made novel — Cooper channeled a remarkable mythopoeic imagination into one of our most enduring myths: that the American, in the words of D. H. Lawrence, is "hard, stoical, isolate, and a killer." Cooper's Natty Bumppo or Deerslayer, epical hero of the "Leather-Stocking" novels, is an incredibly self-righteous patriot, aristocrat of nature, and terror to the wicked red man. Initiated into manhood by murder (not sex), Deerslayer dies in the transfiguring light of heaven. It is not an altogether pretty myth, but it allows us to connect certain alien events in our culture: the latest Lone Ranger shoot-'em-up, for example, with the Gothic horror of Norman Mailer's *Why Are We in Vietnam?* The myth embodies our Puritan heritage, our frontier violence, and the divine rectitude of our manifest destiny.

Cooper's relation to America was ambivalent, compounded of love and hate. Having spent seven years of his maturity abroad, from 1826 to 1833, he returned grieving for America's lost promise — as he saw it, an aristocracy of worth, manners, and land-tenure which had withered in the uncaring hands of the mobocracy and the *nouveaux riches*. Vilified for his conservative notions, but giving as good as he got, Cooper exhausted much of his last years in litigation and in writing sociopolitical propaganda, often disguised as fiction. At the end, he knew that only the Deerslayer series would survive. It has survived despite the sentimental fantasy, melodramatic claptrap, Christian moralism, and highfalutin prose because, as a legible version of what we often are, it interprets us to ourselves.

JOHN WESLEY JARVIS, oil on canvas, 30⅛ x 25, not dated
Lent by Yale University Art Gallery, New Haven, Connecticut

187

GEORGE CATLIN   *Historian of Vanishing Americans*   **1796-1872**

Seeing a delegation of western Indians going through Philadelphia on their way to Washington in the 1820s, George Catlin was overawed by the "silent and stoic dignity of these lords of the forest." He realized sadly that civilization would soon obliterate their grace and nobility, and resolved that "the history and customs of such a people . . . are themes worthy of the life-time of one man, and nothing short of the loss of my life, shall prevent me from visiting their country, and of becoming their historian." Abandoning a successful career as a portrait painter, Catlin spent the rest of his life at his self-appointed task. He traveled widely beyond the Mississippi, completing hundreds of paintings of Indian culture and western scenes, known previously only to fur traders.

Catlin then embarked on a second career of presenting the Indians to the public. A gifted showman, he traveled with his "Indian Gallery," a great exhibition featuring his unique and startling collection. Crowds flocked to see his show and for many it was their first insight into the "Wild West." In Europe, too, he enjoyed a huge success: The collection was exhibited in London and, at the request of King Louis Philippe, in the Louvre. But interest in the paintings soon wore off and the expenses of exhibiting them outran profits.

Heavily in debt, Catlin was forced to sell most of his collection. Although much of his lifework was gone, Catlin started a second collection, recreating many of his earlier paintings from memory. At this time, Joseph Henry, the first Secretary of the Smithsonian Institution, invited him to live at the Institution and exhibit his works. There he continued writing and painting until his death in 1872. In 1879, nearly 450 paintings by Catlin that had survived were donated to the Smithsonian Institution.

WILLIAM FISK, oil on canvas, 49 x 39, 1849
Lent by National Collection of Fine Arts, Smithsonian Institution

NATHANIEL HAWTHORNE *Journalist of the Puritan Soul* **1804-1864**

Nathaniel Hawthorne, in the company of Melville and Poe, best elucidates the power of blackness and the dark side of American experience which issues in pride, sin, and the corrosions of guilt. A descendant of Judge John Hathorne (Nathaniel changed the spelling of the family name) of the Salem witchcraft trials, Hawthorne was haunted by the sanctity of the human soul. To violate it in another, he felt, is to abridge not only the humanity of one's neighbor but of oneself. It is the sin of that Satanist, the mad protopsychiatrist Roger Chillingworth of *The Scarlet Letter* (1850), that he breaks the "magnetic chain" of humankind by invading the private heart of the Reverend Dimmesdale.

Hawthorne was cautious and curious about the discordant springs of human motive. He was wary of those who, like Emerson, asserted the perfectibilty of man, but twice wary of those, represented by Hollings-

worth in *The Blithedale Romance* (1852), who would reform mankind. In *The Marble Faun* (1860) Hawthorne acknowledges the Fall of Man — then, ironically, finds it Fortunate. The vehicle by which he conveyed the ambiguity of the moral universe was allegory, a system of discourse that expresses and coordinates the world of fact and the world of imagination, while at the same time it accommodates itself to the complexity, uncertainty, and obscurity of human experience.

Hawthorne was our first great writer to possess a sense of the past, of that Original Sin which contaminates the present — the curse on the House. In this James and Faulkner are his heirs. Hawthorne's attitude is not entirely pessimistic, however, for in *The House of the Seven Gables* (1851) the curse is lifted through knowledge, perseverance, courage, and love — making that novel, of course, a comedy.

EMANUEL LEUTZE, oil on canvas, oval, 29¾ x 25¼, not dated
Gift of Andrew Mellon   NPG.42.11

HENRY WADSWORTH LONGFELLOW *Poet of the Middle Way* **1807-1882**

Henry Wadsworth Longfellow is the schoolmarm of American letters. The most popular American poet of his day, he immortalized certain aspects of American history and legend — the Indian youth of Hiawatha, the courtship of Miles Standish, and Paul Revere's ride — that we cannot remember in any context save his. Longfellow, who did not attempt a complex or intellectual poetry, wished to reach the commonest man and in fact has succored generations with the simple pieties of "The Psalm of Life" and "Excelsior." His conscientious craftsmanship and the mellifluousness of his verse also helped him to achieve national prominence.

American literature in the nineteenth century was ridden by a sense of its own inferiority. In *Hiawatha* (1855) Longfellow tried to create an American epic which would rival those of other nations. Based in part on a Finnish poem, *Hiawatha* fails because it is transparently derivative and "literary," whereas the first edition of *Leaves of Grass*, which Whitman published in the same year, succeeds magnificently because the Muses heeded Whitman's exhortation to transplant themselves bodily from Greece to America.

Longfellow is the poet of the great indoors — the world of books. His finest inspirations come from literature — from Chaucer and from Dante whom he translated — not from life. Not even prolonged grief over the deaths of two wives, the second in a particularly senseless tragedy, could disturb the scholarly detachment and gentlemanly decorum of his verses. Unlike his greater contemporaries, he could do little with Emerson's "pan and firkin" or Thoreau's Walden, and even less with Melville's South Seas or the rough and tumble of Whitman's New York.

JAMES BUCHANAN READ, oil on canvas, 33 x 27¾, 1869
Lent by Mrs. Thomas Curtis

HERMAN MELVILLE *Grail-Seeker*

At the center of Herman Melville's art is a quest for the sacred; it is his consuming theme, and it very nearly consumed him. In his earliest novel, *Typee* (1846), he discovered not merely the South Seas but a mythical place in the Western imagination, our earthly paradise. After losing it he spent a lifetime trying to regain it.

As Melville matured, the quest became wonderfully elaborated, assuming philosophical, metaphysical, sexual, and sociopolitical dimensions. It spawned one of the most complex novels ever written in America — *Mardi* (1849); one of the bitterest — *Pierre* (1852); one of the most nihilistic — *The Confidence-Man* (1857); and probably the greatest — *Moby Dick* (1851). The White Whale, the supreme multiplex

symbol of our literature, represents divine ultimacy irreducible in meaning; and the questers who seek him represent men faced by our modern predicament: Ahab, whose death admits the futility of questing; Ishmael, whose life admits the necessity.

Toward the end, inspired anew by a "spontaneous aftergrowth" — a psychic conversion toward which he had gradually grown — Melville returned again to the problem that he apparently could not solve. Having died to art, however, he could be reborn. With *Billy Budd* (1890) he regained the sacred isle, for from the tragic merging of the fallible Billy and the God-like Captain Vere issued the divine Budd, the Christ incarnate. *Billy Budd* was the last book Melville wrote — or needed to write.

ASA W. TWITCHELL, oil on canvas, 25 x 21, oval, about 1848
Lent by The Berkshire Athenaeum, Pittsfield, Massachusetts

WALT WHITMAN   *Democracy's Poet-Priest*   **1819-1892**

Walt Whitman is our national and most heroic poet, and *Leaves of Grass* (1855), that enormously vital, fresh, and exuberant book, is our sacred text. Intimately attuned to the cosmic process, Whitman finds within the illuminative mating of body and soul a second Eden of which he is the first citizen — Adam in possession of the land and naming all its parts. He saw himself as father of a new people — courageous, healthy, free — gifted with unlimited possibility and undeterred by the corruption and spiritual paralysis of the Old World.

And yet Whitman is much more complex than a brilliant purveyor of the American Dream or even the celebrant of a perfected democracy. Poet of sexuality, he was homoerotic and unmarried. Poet of the "di-vine average," he was scornful of labor unions. Proclaiming himself one of the roughs, he wore silk underwear. The butterfly on his finger in a famous portrait turned out to be cardboard. Our most innovative and supreme poet, he was suspicious of language and claimed that the United States itself was the greatest poem. Whitman miraculously bridged these disparities and others by twinning a comic to a cosmic consciousness, at once self-reflective and self-reflexive: "By my life-lumps! becoming already a creator!"

Whitman's favorite portrait, here reproduced, is by Thomas Eakins, of whom Whitman said: "Eakins is not a painter, he is a force." The same — and in the same sense — might be said of Whitman, sounder of the "barbaric yawp."

THOMAS EAKINS, oil on canvas, 30 x 24, 1887
Lent by The Pennsylvania Academy of the Fine Arts, Philadelphia, Pennsylvania

STEPHEN COLLINS FOSTER   *Romanticist of the Old South*   **1826-1864**

Most Americans have progressed in understanding of Negro life beyond the sentimentalized image recorded in Stephen Foster's songs, but the popularity of these songs persists. The nostalgia which they express for a South that never was has passed into popular ballad literature where it voices everyone's memory of home and a vanished simplicity.

Foster belonged to a musically gifted Scotch-Irish family. Although he never received extensive musical training, he became the composer of over two hundred songs and instrumental works. He was greatly influenced by the minstrel shows he saw in his childhood home of Pittsburgh and started as a songwriter by composing songs in "darky" dialect for Christy's Minstrels and other troupes. By personal arrangement, E. P. Christy performed and popularized many of Foster's songs often before they were published. The demand for "The Old Folks at Home," the most successful of his minstrel songs, kept three presses running. Negroes and whites alike succumbed to its contagious melancholy.

Foster did not make his first trip to the Deep South until 1852 when he went by steamboat to New Orleans. But memories from his youth had a southern flavor since boats from New Orleans regularly came to Pittsburgh at the head of the Ohio River. Later, in Cincinnati, he was still closer to southern life, for his brother's warehouse, where he worked for a time as bookkeeper, was on the river docks. The Fosters were ardent Democrats and hated the abolitionists, but Stephen's sympathies were with the Union at the outbreak of civil war.

His last years were darkened by total poverty, obscurity, and heavy drinking. The writer of "O Susanna," "Old Black Joe," "Massa's in the Cold Ground," and "My Old Kentucky Home" died in the charity ward at Bellevue Hospital. His epitaph might have been taken from one of his last and best songs, written in New York — "Beautiful Dreamer."

Thomas Hicks, oil on canvas, 30 x 23, not dated
NPG.42.11

THOMAS EAKINS   *Psychological Realist*   **1844-1916**

Thomas Eakins painted what he saw firsthand with relentless candor. After studying at the Pennsylvania Academy of the Fine Arts, Eakins went to Paris for more training, but was little impressed by European art until he traveled to Spain in 1869 and saw the works of the Spanish realists — Velasquez, Ribera, and Goya. Returning to Philadelphia a year later, he enrolled in medical school in order to study anatomy. The structure of the body was Eakins' lifelong preoccupation, but in rebelling against the romanticized depiction of the human figure so fashionable with academic painters of the day he did not substitute mere surface realism. He used to tell his students, "You can copy a thing to a certain limit. Then you must use intellect. . . . Don't copy. Feel the forms."

Eakins united intellect and feeling to create his portraits, which capture the inner character of the sitter — the realism below the literal surface — as well as the physical likeness. In these powerful and penetrating likenesses he produced the finest American portraits of the second half of the nineteenth century. Every figure he painted was a relentlessly honest portrait — particular rather than generalized, individual rather than typical — as in his own self-portrait illustrated here. Painted when Eakins was approaching his sixties, it reveals a man who had suffered much, had seen things with a minimum of illusion, and yet had retained an essential courage and equanimity as well as a touch of ironic humor.

Eakins liked to show his sitters in their everyday surroundings. Consequently, he became one of the first artists in America to portray in a clear, cold light what was considered an unseemly side of life — sports (he followed prizefighting avidly), circuses, surgical operations, and manual labor.

As a teacher at the Pennsylvania Academy of the Fine Arts, Eakins had an extensive influence on a later generation of painters whom he advised:

If America is to produce great painters and if young art students wish to assume a place in the history of the art of their country, their first desire should be to remain in America, to peer deeper into the heart of American life, rather than to spend their time abroad obtaining a superficial view of the art of the Old World.

SELF-PORTRAIT, oil on canvas, 30 x 25, not dated
Lent by National Academy of Design, New York, New York

DAVID BELASCO *Grand Illusionist*   **1853-1931**

"Fortunate the producer who is first on the ground with what the public will be clamoring for next." David Belasco might have said with equal authority that the public will clamor for what an enterprising producer effectively creates. During the first decade of the twentieth century "Belascoism" was the American public's image of all that was admirable in the legitimate theater. It was generally believed that Belasco was propelling our native dramaturgy into a position of international significance.

This San Francisco-born actor, dramatist, director, and producer had no formal schooling past the age of eighteen, when he joined a vagabond company touring up and down the California coast. After years of apprenticeship as an actor and director, he suddenly attained financial and critical success at the age of forty-five with his Civil War play, *The Heart of Maryland*, which premiered in Washington, D. C. During the next decade he scored several theatrical successes — notably with his one-act play *Madame*

Butterfly, which he later passed on to Puccini. By 1907 he had acquired his own theater on West 44th Street.

His life was devoted to the creation of illusion on the stage and off. Uninterested in the intellectual side of drama, he worked at perfecting lighting, acting style, and other technical details in order to astound audiences with the spectacular realism of his "sensation dramas."

Belasco felt a need to carry over into his personal life the same art of illusion he created so painstakingly in the theater. A shock of black hair (later white) falling over his forehead, the Great Man would sit like an Oriental panjandrum in his theater office, wearing a clerical collar in sentimental recollection of his Catholic education as a boy, and speaking softly about the theater. The world he interpreted to America came to be the only one he knew and one Americans have learned to adore — a world of make-believe.

EVERETT SHINN, charcoal on paper, 15 x 11, 1907
Lent by Museum of the City of New York

JOHN PHILIP SOUSA *Pied Piper of the Martial Spirit* 1854-1932

At a concert in 1897 John Philip Sousa raised his white-gloved hand to conduct his band in the first performance of "Stars and Stripes Forever." As the number drew to a close, the flutes, piccolos, cornets, and trombones rose from various spots in the band, marched to the front of the stage, and lined up in military fashion for the dramatic finale. The ovation that followed proclaimed Sousa's marches the musical expression of American patriotism. Conductor of the United States Marine Band for twelve years (1880-1892), Sousa led his own band in this country and abroad for more than a third of a century after that, except for intervals during the Spanish-American War and World War I when he served as a military bandmaster. He applied his talent for composing martial

music to create a "new sound" and a large audience for band music that has continued to the present day.

In addition to writing many of our most cherished military marches, Sousa was one of the first bandmasters to play the cakewalk and ragtime; and in the 1920s he added syncopated jazz to his programs. He was also a pioneer composer for the American popular stage. With more than a hundred marches, ten comic operas, and innumerable songs, waltzes, overtures, and suites to his credit, Sousa considered himself primarily an entertainer. In actuality much of his music embodied the spirit of an America beginning to attain full growth — strong, self-confident, exuberant, and ingenuous.

HARRY FRANKLIN WALTMAN, oil on canvas, 27⅛ x 22, 1909
Lent by Mrs. Helen Sousa Abert

FLORENZ ZIEGFELD *Designer of Dreams* **1869-1932**

"If Ziegfeld dies, sell Western Union short," a wit once observed, for Ziegfeld was fond of thousand-word telegrams. When he wanted to go camping — "the simple life, that's the ticket," he remarked — he bought an island. He gave mammoth parties at home and had three golden telephones on his office desk. Ziegfeld lived as extravagantly as he knew how — which is to say that the celebrated "Ziegfeld Follies" were merely the public counterpart of his private self.

Florenz Ziegfeld established a high standard for the musical review, and therein lies his particular contribution to American show business. He perfected the art of theatrical presentation, offering new achievements in pageantry, with lavish costumes and settings and beautiful "show girls" whose long-legged semi-nudity set a new style in feminine beauty. From 1907 to 1931 he offered twenty-two "Follies," and in his hard-driving, superbly self-confident, American perfectionist way he employed the best composers and comedians money could buy. He was a star-maker, quick to recognize and publicize undiscovered talent. The first "Follies" featured his first wife, Anna Held, the reigning European beauty whom he celebrated for her milk baths; but Ziegfeld was also instrumental in launching the careers of W. C. Fields, Eddie Cantor, Fanny Brice, Will Rogers, and many other American entertainers. In the American heyday leading up to and following World War I Ziegfeld was an arbiter of popular elegance and the high priest of public entertainment. But he outlived his era: The Depression and newer audiences made his kind of entertainment old-fashioned. The man with three golden telephones died half a million dollars in debt.

UNIDENTIFIED ARTIST, bronze, 20⅝ high, including base, not dated
Gift of an anonymous donor NPG.66.44

GEORGE BELLOWS *Painter of Humanity*

1882-1925

George Bellows' insistent Americanism made him one of the most characteristically "native" American painters. Absorbing his country affectionately, he was preoccupied with the common, good things in life; and his paintings reflect the energy, humor, and gusto of the beginning of the twentieth century. His was an art of the people — warm, compassionate, filled with humanity. His critics said he painted "ugly," "crude" subjects; indeed, his pictures capture pungent scenes of prizefights, religious revivals, and New York's swarming streets. Compared to the "Homeric bard who sang to his fellows of the things they liked to remember," he was an interpreter of the city and everyday life, attuned to the new social and cultural patterns of his day. His unflinching pictures of World War I scenes are among the best to come out of that debacle.

Bellows — affable, self-assured, yet rebelliously independent — painted exactly as he pleased, and paid no heed to what was lucrative or fashionable. Although a "social realist," he followed no school of art. He did not study in Europe, as American artists had traditionally done, but preferred the teaching of Robert Henri, leader in New York of "the Eight" — a new group of American realists. With these he participated in the 1913 Armory Show, which introduced Americans to the best examples of contemporary international art. Vital and robust in nature, Bellows was a professional baseball player who switched to painting as a career. His vigorous, honest paintings soon brought him success; but his career ended abruptly when he died at forty-three.

ROBERT HENRI, oil on canvas, 32 x 26, 1911
Lent by National Academy of Design, New York, New York

SINCLAIR LEWIS   *Deliverer from the Philistines*   1885-1951

All his life Sinclair Lewis pursued the "reality" of America — and produced a litany of derogation. Like other more conservative or reactionary Midwesterners — such as Frank Lloyd Wright and Ezra Pound — Lewis compared the America he knew to the America he imagined. He was a critic who rejected a romanticization of "Gopher Prairie" as others before and after him rejected small-town America: as Herman Melville rejected "Saddle Meadows," New York; Sherwood Anderson, "Winesburg," Ohio; and Truman Capote, "Holcomb," Kansas.

For each of his books Lewis did elaborate research, and his style is not without a reportorial flavor. But at his best — in *Main Street* (1920) and *Babbitt* (1922) — his indictment of cultural backwardness, rural inflexibility, and spiritual and intellectual impoverishment establishes an imaginative presentation of mid-

western life that the Lynds' famous sociological study of "Middletown" cannot match. Lewis found targets everywhere: in *Arrowsmith* (1925), the complacency and hypocrisy of the medical profession in its least noble aspect; in *Elmer Gantry* (1927), the provinciality and deceptiveness of evangelical religion.

One of his most interesting and least-read books, written at the height of the Depression, is *It Can't Happen Here* (1935), which deals with a fascist regime elected democratically in the United States. The new President, backed by storm troopers called "Minute Men," gerrymanders the country into eight sectors and deprives the Legislative and Judicial branches of their power. At one point Lewis' protagonist is confined to a concentration camp. Reading the book today, one is made newly aware of the power of art both to prophesy and to legislate life.

Jo Davidson, bronze, 20 high, including base, not dated
NPG.68.9

Idols

The American has had a greater need of freshly manufactured idols than have members of older cultures and
more stratified societies. Lacking roots himself, he is
cynical about heroes of other generations; focusing on the
future as shaped by current ideals, he needs an image of
what he's going to be "when he grows up" — "when he
makes his pile."

Most Americans discover thir idols in the marketplace,
prepackaged like soup and soap. "Show-biz" merges into
politics, and a good promotion agency can make a popular
hero of the most unpromising material. Unlike countries
where pageantry, ceremony, and titles are provided by
state and church, America looks for its idols in the ephem-
eral world of entertainment and sports. Only when the
nation is engaged in war or its peacetime equivalent, an
election campaign, does an occasional military figure or
politician enter the popularity contest. Whatever his role,
the national idol must be someone with whom the average
American man or woman can imagine changing places.

In this country of rapid change and social mobility the
idol's life expectancy has always been brief. But with the
recent worship of youth and flamboyance, and with the
supersaturation of the public by the mass media, idols —
like everything else in our consumer economy — fall victim to planned obsolescence. The various beauty and
popularity queens — Miss (and Mrs.) America, Miss
United States, Miss Teen-Ager, Miss Meat-Packer, ad
libitum — are folk goddesses whose life cycles are completed in a single year. In other cultures a pretty young
"cat" may look at a king or hope to marry a prince; here
her sweetest dream is to reign briefly as a voluntary sacrifice to American materialism and fickleness.

EDWIN FORREST *Actor in the Grand Style* **1806-1872**

Edwin Forrest is commonly regarded as America's first great actor. He was grandly eloquent, according to contemporary reports, and was a distinguished tragedian of heroic proportion. In a picturesque, richly oratorical style he played all the major Shakespearian roles as well as those written especially for him. Although he was not without fault as an actor — he occasionally ranted — he was never without success. From the age of twenty, when he made a successful New York debut as Othello, until his retirement he made large sums from his performances.

Forrest took great pride in his country — he regarded himself as a man of its people, brought his theater to its remote regions, and inveighed against aristocratic arrogance with his own democratic boastfulness. It was probably xenophobia — made worse by

jealousy of a competent rival — that was responsible for his openly hissing the English Shakespearian actor William Macready; and Forrest was at least indirectly responsible for stirring his followers to riot at a Macready performance at which twenty-two persons were killed. As an actor, Forrest of course courted publicity, but one wonders if the Macready scandal, like his protracted and widely publicized divorce suit, was not an act of exhibitionism. His powerful portrayals of strong-willed, elemental characters were matched only by his own egocentric, passionate nature. In his last years, after being congratulated for his playing of King Lear, Forrest indignantly and without irony replied: *"Play Lear!* What do you mean, sir, I do not *play Lear!* . . . by God, sir, I *am Lear!"*

DAVID JOHNSON, oil on canvas, 24⅛ x 20⅛, 1871
Lent by the National Gallery of Art, Washington, D. C.

CHARLOTTE CUSHMAN *Reigning Stage Queen* **1816-1876**

In the age of classic acting Charlotte Cushman stood out as the first lady of the American theater, the first American actress to attain international acclaim, and one of the finest tragediennes of the nineteenth century.

A tall, sturdy woman, without great beauty, she brought to the stage the earnestness and determination of her Boston Puritan ancestors. With these qualities she combined intelligence, a voice of remarkable flexibility, and a painstaking mastery of stage technique that enabled her to enthrall other performers as well as audiences.

Charlotte Cushman made her stage debut in 1835. After playing in repertory theater in New York and Philadelphia, she accepted the suggestion of the visiting English actor William Macready that she go to London to complete her apprenticeship. There, between 1845 and her return to the United States in 1849, she became a celebrated actress. Her tours of America won her critical acclaim and affection which continued long after her semiretirement in 1858.

Although she occasionally played male roles, notably that of Romeo, her greatest successes were as Lady Macbeth, as Queen Katherine in Shakespeare's *Henry VIII*, and as Meg Merrilies and Nancy Sykes in dramatizations of Scott's *Guy Mannering* and *Oliver Twist*.

THOMAS SULLY, oil on canvas, 20 x 17½, 1843
Lent by Library Company of Philadelphia

GEORGE ARMSTRONG CUSTER *Boy Wonder*   1839-1876

On 25 June 1876 Lieutenant Colonel George Armstrong Custer, commanding the 7th United States Cavalry, rode down a ridge in Montana and passed from history into legend. The change, however, was almost imperceptible, for Custer was already legendary. At the Little Big Horn the warriors of Sitting Bull and Crazy Horse crowned the career of a national hero with a suitably epic death.

"Armstrong" — as his family called him — was born in Ohio, graduated from West Point, and commissioned a second lieutenant in 1861. During the Civil War, when many dashing cavalry officers were capturing the public imagination, Custer became one of the most glamorous and popular. At the age of twenty-five, as a breveted major general, he was credited with a decisive role in forcing Robert E. Lee's surrender.

In 1866 Custer went to the West, where in the next ten years the golden-haired young general became the paladin of the plains, feared by Indians and disliked by politicians. The reports of journalists who visited him and the accounts in his own book, *My Life on the Plains* (1874), made Custer a national idol. His tragic last stand and the mystery surrounding it sealed the legend.

MATHEW BRADY, photograph, 5¾ x 3⅞, not dated
Lent by the Library of Congress

COL. W. F. CODY. "BUFFALO BILL."

Stacy WILD WEST CORNER 9TH ST. & 5TH AVE. BROOKLYN.

BUFFALO BILL CODY   *Flower of Knighthood*   **1846-1917**

When the real West was tamed late in the nineteenth century the Wild West of romance took its place. Dime novels peopled the Plains with hard-riding straight-shooting heroes, cattle rustlers, stagecoach bandits, and Indian war parties. Buffalo Bill's appeal rested on this nostalgia for an American equivalent of Camelot. He was the dime-novel hero come to life.

Fiction embroidered Cody's exploits and invented new ones, but behind the fiction was hard fact. Born in Iowa as William Frederick Cody, he was raised on the Indian frontier, served for a time as a pony-express rider, and became an accomplished buffalo-hunter,

scout, and Indian fighter. He was already well known when he began appearing in stage westerns — forerunners of western movies and television series — in the 1870s. In 1883 he formed his Wild West Show, a combination circus and traveling museum of the West. Audiences watched real cowboys chase — and be chased by — real Indians; gazed at buffalo; and thrilled to exhibitions of roping, bronco-busting, and the sharpshooting of Annie Oakley. Through his show Buffalo Bill carried the romance of western life across America and western Europe.

STACY, cabinet photograph, 6½ x 4¼, not dated
Lent by the Library of Congress

JOHN L. SULLIVAN *The Boston Strong Boy* **1858-1918**

The "Great John L." Sullivan, one of the most popular prizefighters of all time, was America's first great sports hero. Crowds flocked to see the invincible boxer. Launching his professional boxing career at nineteen, he knocked his first opponent into the orchestra with his "knock-em-dead" punch. Blatantly confident, he hammered his opponents into unconsciousness with his bare fists; his bout with Jake Kilrain, the last professional bare-knuckle fight, went seventy-five rounds. In 1882 he knocked out Paddy Ryan in nine rounds to win the American championship, which he held for ten years. He was world champion for three years.

Habituating saloons, Sullivan's life outside the arena was riotous, and he spent little time in training. In 1892 when he met with James L. Corbett — the nimble-footed, well-conditioned antithesis of the now flabby and dissipated Sullivan — he was defeated in the twenty-first round. This defeat ended Sullivan's career as a prizefighter; he fell into debt and drifted into vaudeville, touring the United States and Canada. Finally giving up drink, he became a temperance lecturer in 1905. His last days were spent in poverty on a farm in Massachusetts where he lived with an old sparring partner.

J. M. MORA, photograph, 13 x 7½, 1882
Lent by the Library of Congress

LILLIAN RUSSELL   *Darling of the Gay Nineties*   **1861-1922**

Lillian Russell was the prima donna of the American musical theater at the end of the nineteenth century. From Clinton, Iowa, where she was born as Helen Louise Leonard, she went to New York to study voice under Leopold Damrosch. She made a rather unpromising debut — as the "English Ballad Singer" — at the Tony Pastor Music Hall in 1880. Five years later she rose to stardom in the comic opera *Polly*. For the next twenty years, as the comely ingenue of comic operas and as the star of the Weber and Fields burlesque shows, she reigned supreme. While doing so, she helped establish Broadway as the glamorous

Great White Way, and the shows built around her were forerunners of the more sophisticated revues and musical comedies of the twentieth century.

Lillian Russell possessed a clear, cool soprano voice. But to those who never heard her sing it was her beauty and elegance in dress that made her a national idol. Men admired the combination of sweet face and buxom, hourglass figure — a paradox that suggested girlish innocence in a womanly body. Her gowns, hats, and jewels, aped by women, set the carriage-trade fashion at the turn of the century.

ADOLFO MULLER-URY, pastel on ecru board, 26 x 16, not dated
Lent by Jessica Dragonette

FIORELLO LA GUARDIA   *The Little Flower*   **1882-1947**

Fiorello La Guardia was a man of the people. With Italian parents, and able to speak Yiddish, Italian, and English, he represented and championed the "new immigrants" who swarmed into America after the 1880s. As Congressman (1916-1919, 1923-1933) and as mayor of New York City (1934-1945) he was a liberal reformer who combined a sincere devotion to public service with the cunning of a ward politician. He anticipated New Deal humanitarianism with his prolabor and social welfare programs. His honest reform government, nonpartisanship, and ability to get things done made him one of the political masters of his generation.

Theatrical and impulsive, La Guardia was one of New York's most colorful and popular figures. He was fiercely competitive and often belligerent and irascible; his strong desire to be on top made him fight hard for power and fame. Yet his warmhearted-

ness, good nature, and sense of the comic endeared him to myriad followers. He was seldom seen without his corncob pipe and black fedora, and his short, round figure was a familiar sight around New York. He was an exuberant showman: His amusing and engaging antics — chasing after fires, hanging his wash in the yard of Gracie Mansion, or reading the comic strips over the radio during a newspaper strike—made him seem all the more accessible to his people.

In this photograph La Guardia is seen reading the New York *Daily Mirror* for 17 September 1941, in which his victory in the Republican mayoralty primary is announced. In the lower right corner of the newspaper is a photograph showing Archbishop Francis J. Spellman, Governor Herbert Lehman, and Mayor La Guardia at the Fordham University centennial celebration in the Waldorf Astoria Hotel.

PHOTOGRAPH, 7⅞ x 6⅛, 17 September 1941

JIM THORPE *All-American Athlete*   **1888-1953**

James Thorpe, an American Indian who was proficient at almost every sport, became one of the greatest all-around athletes in American sports history. While he was at the Carlisle Indian School, in Pennsylvania, his coach — "Pop" Warner — developed him into a powerful football and track star. Representing the United States in the Olympic Games of 1912, he held the spotlight by winning with ease both the pentathlon and decathlon — both requiring competition in a number of events. The peak of his career came when King Gustav V of Sweden told him, "You, sir, are the greatest athlete in the world."

Misfortune followed Thorpe's victories at the Olympics, however. In the following year it was discovered that he had played semiprofessional baseball in the summer of 1911. Although he had been paid only twenty-five dollars a week as a ballplayer, he had automatically forfeited his eligibility for amateur competition. As a result his gold medals and trophies were taken from him and his Olympic Games records erased from the books. For a time he tried to make the most of his professionalism by playing professional football and baseball, but only two years after his retirement in 1929 he was found working for four dollars a day with a pick and shovel. He began to drink heavily, and drifted from job to job. In 1950 he sold the movie rights to his life story for $1,500. Two years later he died alone in a trailer outside Los Angeles, but the film had made him immortal.

PHOTOGRAPH, 8 x 6, not dated

RUDOLPH VALENTINO *Mythical Lover*   **1895-1926**

Few of the women who twisted their damp handkerchiefs during Rudolph Valentino's performances on the silent screen would have believed that he owed his success to an unaffected, ingenuous personality. The great lover came to America from Italy to be a farmer; he became a movie star only because he could not make the down payment for a parcel of land in California. His fortune was made in the film world after a director discovered that he could convey primitive passion and animal intensity with a minimum of histrionics. Valentino was a born actor who lived his unvarying roles with absolute conviction.

With the tango as his trademark, and with his dark good looks and childlike delight in exotic costumes, he could send females in his audience into ecstacy. Although his repertory of facial expression never went beyond a veiled look from his deep-set, almond eyes or a gleaming smile of pure joy, his bold direct approach to the weaker sex in *The Sheik* and similar roles made women from nine to ninety forget their respectable, humdrum lives.

EDWARD STEICHEN, photograph, 10 x 8, August 1926
Lent by Edward Steichen

BABE RUTH *Home-Run King*   **1895-1948**

To a generation disenchanted with war, politics, and grand ideals, the physical prowess of George Herman Ruth had an appeal that was immediate and universal. Dubbed by various sportswriters as "Sultan of Swat," "King of Clout," and "The Bambino," Babe Ruth became the greatest slugger and one of the most colorful players baseball has known. His numerous, powerful home-run hits filled stadiums with spectators and helped transform baseball from a national game into a popular and lucrative industry.

At the same time Ruth symbolized the American rags-to-riches dream. From the obscurity of a Roman Catholic boys' home in Baltimore he became first a star pitcher for the Boston Red Sox and then super-star outfielder of the New York Yankees. At the peak of his career he was paid more than the President of the United States — and was as well known. Money and fame, however, never destroyed his down-to-earth, exuberant humanity. To millions of common men he has always remained one of their own kind who had made good.

PHOTOGRAPH, 5 x 6, 29 April 1920

JEAN HARLOW   *Blond Bombshell*   1911-1937

Each generation in America has produced its living symbols of female beauty and allure — personifications of an ideal at once accessible and unattainable. Since the advent of motion pictures these female idols have been largely Hollywood-created. In the first decade of the motion picture industry, the "vamp" — Theda Bara, Vilma Banky, Clara Kimball Young — represented every tired businessman's dream of the unscrupulous, seductive woman who leads willing men to their ruin. The war generation of the forties produced the GI's "pin-up" — a combination of the girl back home and a mythical camp follower — in the glamorous persons of such stars as Betty Grable, Jane Russell, Anne Sheridan, Rita Hayworth, Lauren Bacall. In the intervening heyday of the thirties the cool, poised, self-reliant woman of the world appeared. Alternately an aloof glamor girl and a companionable comedienne, she was typified by Carole Lombard, Myrna Loy, Dolores Del Rio, Claudette Colbert, Lupe Velez — but by none more memorably than Jean Harlow.

The facts of Jean Harlow's life correspond closely to the fictional "life stories" manufactured by movie studios for their actresses. She registered at the Central Casting Bureau during a chance visit to Fox Film studios and got her big opportunity when Howard Hughes chose her for *Hell's Angels* (1930) after deciding to make it a talking picture instead of a silent film.

Harlow's success was immediate because in the world of the silver screen she projected a bright, metallic image of flawless beauty, emancipated morality, and snappy repartee that made her equal to any occasion — or to any man. Every young girl longing to emulate her rushed to the nearest drug store for peroxide to duplicate the star's famous platinum blonde hair. Her classic beauty and her understated, relaxed acting were spiced by a flair for comedy and a frank sexual awareness — which kept the censors wary but appealed to the increasing sophistication of American audiences. Like Valentino, she died at the height of fame, before age could tarnish her glittering image.

PHOTOGRAPH, 10 x 8, not dated
Lent by The Museum of Modern Art, Department of Film, New York, New York

THE OREGON TRAIL
by ALBERT BIERSTADT
Oil on canvas, 31 x 49, 1869
Lent by The Butler Institute of American Art
Youngstown, Ohio

THE COUNTY ELECTION
by GEORGE CALEB BINGHAM
Oil on canvas, 35½ x 48¾, 1851-1852
Lent by City Art Museum of Saint Louis
Saint Louis, Missouri

THE LAST MOMENTS OF JOHN BROWN
by THOMAS HOVENDEN
Oil on canvas, 77⅜ x 63¼, 1884
Lent by The Metropolitan Museum of Art
Gift of Mr. and Mrs. Carl Stoeckel, 1897

EXHUMING THE FIRST AMERICAN MASTODON
by CHARLES WILLSON PEALE
Oil on canvas, 50 x 62½, 1806
Lent by The Peale Museum, Baltimore, Maryland
Gift of Mrs. Harry White in memory of her husband

MEN OF PROGRESS
by CHRISTIAN SCHUSSELE
Oil on canvas, 51⅜ x 78¾, 1862
Gift of Andrew Mellon, 1942   NPG.42.20

IN THE LAND OF PROMISE; CASTLE GARDENS
by CHARLES F. ULRICH
Oil on panel, 28⅜ x 35¾, 1884
Lent by the Corcoran Gallery of Art
Washington, D. C.

WASHINGTON IRVING AND HIS FRIENDS AT SUNNYSIDE
by CHRISTIAN SCHUSSELE
Oil on canvas, 48 x 72, 1863
Lent by Sleepy Hollow Restorations, Tarrytown, New York

HOMAGE TO EAKINS
by RAPHAEL SOYER
Oil on canvas, 88 x 80, 1964-1965
Lent by Joseph H. Hirshhorn Foundation

GRANT AND HIS GENERALS
by OLE PETER HANSEN BALLING
Oil on canvas, 120 x 192, 1864-1865
Gift of Mrs. Harry Newton Blue   NPG.66.37

WILLIAM JENNINGS BRYAN
by IRVING R. WILES
Oil on canvas, 60 x 40, 1917
Lent by Department of State, Washington, D.C.

FREDERICK DOUGLASS
by an unidentified artist, 26 x 17½, not dated
Lent by the Rhode Island Historical Society,
Providence, Rhode Island

Opening Exhibition Committee

Edward H. Dwight
Edgar P. Richardson
Charles Nagel
Daniel J. Reed
Virginia C. Purdy
Robert G. Stewart
Riddick Vann

Lenders to the Exhibition

Abby Aldrich Rockefeller Folk Art Collection, Williamsburg, Virginia
Mrs. Helen Sousa Abert
Addison Gallery of American Art, Andover, Massachusetts
Allen Memorial Art Museum, Oberlin College, Oberlin, Ohio
American Antiquarian Society, Worcester, Massachusetts
Mrs. Julia L. Asher
The Baltimore Museum of Art, Baltimore, Maryland
August Belmont
The Berkshire Athenaeum, Pittsfield, Massachusetts
Mrs. George Brooke III
The Brooklyn Museum, Brooklyn, New York
Jonathan Bryan
The Butler Institute of Art, Youngstown, Ohio
California Institute of Technology, Pasadena, California
Chicago Historical Society, Chicago, Illinois
City Art Museum of Saint Louis, Saint Louis, Missouri
City of Boston, Boston, Massachusetts
Corcoran Gallery of Art, Washington, D. C.
Mrs. Thomas Curtis
Department of State, Washington, D. C.
The Detroit Institute of Arts, Detroit, Michigan
Mrs. John Dewey
Miss Jessica Dragonette
The Enoch Pratt Free Library, Baltimore, Maryland
Field Enterprises, Inc., Chicago, Illinois
Fogg Art Museum, Harvard University, Cambridge, Massachusetts
Georgetown University, Washington, D. C.
Mr. and Mrs. F. Woodson Hancock
Harper Memorial Library, University of Chicago, Chicago, Illinois
The Hearst Corporation, San Francisco, California
Hebrew Union College, Cincinnati, Ohio
Joseph H. Hirshhorn Foundation, New York, New York
Independence National Historical Park Collection, Philadelphia,
    Pennsylvania
Jane Addams' Hull House, University of Illinois, Chicago, Illinois
Mrs. Peter A. Jay
Kunstmuseum, Basel, Switzerland
Kunstmuseum, Berne, Switzerland
Mrs. Cazenove Lee
Maurice du Pont Lee
Library Company of Philadelphia, Philadelphia, Pennsylvania
Library of Congress, Washington, D. C.
The Mariners Museum, Newport News, Virginia
Massachusetts Historical Society, Boston, Massachusetts
Mayo Foundation, Rochester, Minnesota
Methodist Historical Society, Lovely Lane Museum, Baltimore, Maryland
The Metropolitan Museum of Art, New York, New York

Missouri Historical Society, St. Louis, Missouri
Montclair Art Museum, Montclair, New Jersey
Museum der Stadt Solothurn, Solothurn, Switzerland
Museum of Art, Carnegie Institute, Pittsburgh, Pennsylvania
Museum of Fine Arts, Boston, Massachusetts
Museum of Modern Art, New York, New York
The Museum of Science, Boston, Massachusetts
Museum of the City of New York, New York, New York
National Academy of Design, New York, New York
National Carl Schurz Association, Inc., Philadelphia, Pennsylvania
National Collection of Fine Arts, Smithsonian Institution,
    Washington, D. C.
National Gallery of Art, Washington, D. C.
National Portrait Gallery, London
National Trust for Historic Preservation, Washington, D. C.
New York Chamber of Commerce, New York, New York
The New-York Historical Society, New York, New York
New York State Historical Association, Cooperstown, New York
North Carolina Museum of Art, Raleigh, North Carolina
Mr. and Mrs. Garrison Norton
The Orchestral Association, Chicago, Illinois
Potter Palmer
Peabody Museum, Salem, Massachusetts
The Peale Museum, Baltimore, Maryland
The Pennsylvania Academy of Fine Arts, Philadelphia, Pennsylvania
Philadelphia Museum of Art, Philadelphia, Pennsylvania
Mrs. Frederic R. Pratt
Joseph Pulitzer, Jr.
Reorganized Church of Jesus Christ of Latter Day Saints,
    Independence, Missouri
Rhode Island Historical Society, Providence, Rhode Island
Mr. and Mrs. Benjamin Rush
Saint Elizabeths Hospital, Washington, D. C.
Mrs. Wharton Sinkler
G. Richard Slade
Sleepy Hollow Restorations, Tarrytown, New York
Edward Steichen
Teachers College, Columbia University, New York, New York
Texas Library and Historical Commission, Texas State Library,
    Austin, Texas
Theatre Collection of the New York Public Library,
    New York, New York
The Thoreau Society and the Concord Free Public Library,
    Concord, Massachusetts
Tufts University, Medford, Massachusetts
The Honorable William R. Tyler
University of Pennsylvania, Philadelphia, Pennsylvania
Mrs. Alan Valentine
Vanderbilt University, Nashville, Tennessee
The Virginia Museum of Fine Arts, Richmond, Virginia
Chauncey L. Waddell
Walters Art Gallery, Baltimore, Maryland
Washington and Lee University, Lexington, Virginia
The Western Reserve Historical Society, Cleveland, Ohio
Yale University Art Gallery, New Haven, Connecticut

The following individuals and institutions kindly loaned objects associated with the exhibition:

The Peale Museum, Baltimore, Maryland

Museum of Comparative Zoology, Harvard University,
Cambridge, Massachusetts

Dr. Charles Coleman Sellers

The Library of Congress, Washington, D. C.

National Aeronautics and Space Administration, Washington, D. C.

Museum of History and Technology, Smithsonian Institution,
Washington, D. C.

Museum of Natural History, Smithsonian Institution, Washington, D. C.

Mrs. Kenneth R. Higgins

The American National Red Cross, Washington, D. C.

The Synagogue Architectural Library of the Union of American
Hebrew Congregations, New York, New York

Christian Science Committee on Publication, Washington, D. C.

National Park Service, Washington, D. C.

Senator Ralph D. Yarborough, Texas

Senator Thomas H. Kuchel, California

Hammacher-Schlemmer, New York, New York

Theatre Collection of the New York Public Library